SELF-SABOTAGING FEARS:

THE DREAM DESTROYERS

DEBBIE KING MABRAY,
MS, LMFT, LPC, CART

PublishAmerica
Baltimore

First printing

At the specific preference of the author, PublishAmerica allowed this work to remain exactly as the author intended, verbatim, without editorial input.

ISBN: 1-4241-3241-X
PUPUBLISHED BY PUBLISHAMERICA, LLLP
www.publishamerica.com
Baltimore

Printed in the United States of America

Table of Contents

Motivational Quotes

The significant problems we face today cannot be solved at the same level of thinking we were at when we created them.
—Albert Einstein

Tell me and I'll forget; show me and I may remember; involve me and I'll understand.
—Chinese Proverb

Perhaps the reward of the spirit who tries is not the goal but the exercise.
—E. V. Cooke

To be what we are, and to become what we are capable of becoming, is the only end in life.
—Baruch Spinoza

I have been absolutely terrified every moment of my life and I've never let it keep me from doing a single thing that I wanted to do.
—Georgia O'Keefe

A journey of a thousand miles must begin with a single step.
—Chinese Proverb

Procrastination is opportunity's natural assassin.
—Victor Kiam

Knowing is not enough; we must apply. Willing is not enough; we must do.
—Goethe

What is necessary to change a person is to change his awareness of himself.
—Abraham H. Maslow

Given the right fertilizer, any tomato can win an award.
—Sidney David King

Fears: Ties That Bind

Fear can stop us from entering into something dangerous. Fear is an emotion that, if used properly, should protect us from danger. Fear of jumping in front of a moving car saves our life. Fear of addiction keeps us away from drugs, alcohol, gambling, even excessive shopping or eating. It is natural to experience fear, a basic human emotion. At the core of our psyche, theorists ascertain that we all experience a fear or a fight or flight mechanism. Once again, this is engrained into keeping us safe. This book addresses the other fears. The ones born of early years and experiences. The fears that live within us all and act as barriers to success and actualization. These fears are the sabotaging fears.

An illustration of the difference between the intenseness and severity of the two types of fears discussed involves a fourteen-year-old adolescent told by her mother to find and retrieve a flat, circular rock from the front yard. The mother is constructing a centerpiece for the dinner table.

The girl sorts through many rocks in the front yard while the mother is yelling, "I am in a hurry. Move it!"

A rock that is flat but not symmetrically circular is located. Two others, which are similar, are also collected. Beneath the rocks is a nonpoisonous snake. Primal fear makes the girl back up, carefully avoiding the snake as to not be injured.

Carrying the rocks into the house, she is dismayed when her mother says, "You are so stupid. You'll never do anything right. These are not large enough to help me in any way. What a loser."

The sabotaging fears of rejection and failure are created within the girl. The teen will easily move on from the snake incident. The degradation from her mother, announcing her current and imminent repetition of failure, creates a baggage that she will carry for sometime.

Sigmund Freud, a psychoanalyst, theorized that our early childhood experiences shape whom we become as adults. A barrage of developmental theorist concurs with this statement. We believe that in addition to this, in order to assist an individual in overcoming their sabotaging fear(s) the therapist must first identify what the fear is. Then, we search for the origination of the fear. Where was it born? What variables combined to create a fertile soil for the fear's growth? Who planted this seed? Why was it never eradicated? How has this fear sabotaged the individual's life thus far? Once these questions are addressed, we can establish a plan of removal.

This book looks at a number of prevalent sabotaging fears. We also explore removal techniques. As always, it is advisable to experience this journey with the aid of a licensed therapist. When the excavation of sabotaging fears has begun, there are often associated issues and barricades that emerge. It is often observed that the fears exist plurally, not alone. This book is not intended to be a quick fix, but rather a starting point to explore causation of behavior and create a movement toward a life free of booby-traps and self-sabotage.

Fear = Exploitations

Once an individual has developed a sabotaging fear, those close to the person are aware. This fear is worn for all to see as if it were a large piece of jewelry adorning the individual. This is obvious to those in close proximity to you, but it even becomes obvious to those you interact with only occasionally. This emblem of fear is an emblem of weakness. It is through manipulation of the fear that people can control your behavior. Some examples of this are:

Scenario #1

A couple is recently married. They move to a country overseas. The female has a *fear of abandonment*. Her husband, in his efforts to compel her to do as he wishes, threatens to "send you home to your parents if you can't tow the line". The woman is immediately thrown into an abyss of terror. Although she may feel extreme anger and resentment, the fear of being alone and the *fear of rejection* of a doomed marriage is more than she can take. She immediately acquiesces. He becomes the partner-in-charge, the parent-like figure. She becomes the child-like figure.

Scenario #2

A couple has been married for fifteen years. The male wishes to return to college to further his career options. His wife is very insecure about this choice. She is afraid if he becomes more knowledgeable or successful, then he will leave her (*fear of abandonment*). Her insecurities propel her to say things like, "You are too old to go back to school. People will call you an old fool."

"Who do you think you are? Do you think you are so much better than me that you should be the one to go to college? What about me? When is it my turn?"

"You can't make it at college. You are not smart enough to succeed in college."

In both cases, the sabotaging fear of one spouse attacks the sabotaging fear of the other. Both partners are miserable, each person's fears are being magnified, and both parties lose. Fear sniffs out weakness, which sniffs out fear. It's a negative cycle that must be broken in order to move ahead in a positive bent. These sabatogers not only destroy an individual but also can easily capsize a marriage.

Exploiting the fear of an individual makes them weak. They cannot respond appropriately because they are reliving the fear and origination causations. In scenario #1, the wife is relieving the earlier life experiences of intense loneliness. The times when she had no friends, no boyfriends. She wanted to be popular, but was ridiculed. Her dream that got her through these early years of torment was the "knight on a white horse", coming to take her away and live happily ever after. Now her knight says she is not good enough for him. He is going to send her home to the perpetual loneliness and inevitable replay of her earlier years. She also believes that she must live with the knowledge that people around her are aware that she is once again not good enough and has been unable to maintain a marriage. She feels failure from her childhood years and failure from her adult years. Her husband, the knight, due to these failures, also abandons her.

In scenario #2, the husband can easily give up on his ambition of success. At some point he believed he was capable of succeeding at college at this point in his life. He obviously thought he could complete the required studies in a positive manner. His wife has wiped out this belief. She is capitalizing on his *fear of failure*. She sees that he is in a precarious state, unsure of what to do. This is the perfect time to create a solid tether around his neck so he doesn't stray. Her *fear of abandonment* directs her to capitalize on his *fear of failure*. If she can disable his drive for advancement, she can keep him at home with her. This is another situation when no one wins. Both are held hostage by their fears. She is exploiting and capitalizing fro m his fear. This is not a healthy relationship.

Guilt can become a factor in sabotaging fears. Baseless accusations, aimed at someone deemed an adversary, directed at their sabotaging fear, can have catastrophic effects. The old adage states," the first one to accuse is the one who did the deed."

When a person carries guilt and self-perceived inadequacies, their sabotaging fears are often substantial. These individuals continually attempt to "get a leg up" on the identified victim by placing themselves in the victim's role. This individual is likely to create allegations, against the real victim, aimed at the real victim's sabotaging fear.

By making the real victim a "bad guy" to observers, the accuser renders him ineffective and powerless.

Example:

Nine-year-old Chrissy is not part of the popular crowd at her elementary school. Her parents cannot afford the name-brand clothing worn by her peers. One of the "popular girls," as a joke, pretended to be Chrissy's friend. Chrissy shared the pain of ostrasization with her, and how she struggles daily just to make it to school with all of the teasing. The popular girl then falsely accuses Chrissy of trying to steal her boyfriend. She tells everyone at school that Chrissy tried to take him away from her, that Chrissy was not a loyal friend, and that Chrissy talked badly about all of them.

This example illustrates how someone used Chrissy's sabotaging *fear of abandonment* to attack her. By attacking Chrissy with false accusations, driving people further from her, she was immobilized. Her fear of abandonment was amplified so intensely, she was unable to strike back. Chrissy had actually been vulnerable to exploitation; the girl capitalized on this and ravaged Chrissy. Chrissy was unable to defend herself in any manner. Emotionally, Chrissy's first instinct would be to crawl in a corner, in a fetal position, protecting herself from the cruel world.

Let's also look at the initiater of Chrissy's ordeal. Why would another person, regardless of age, have the need to be so mean to another? What did the initiater get out of this? She received attention from others that she could manipulate to resemble respect. She was a hero for protecting her boyfriend and girlfriends from the gossip of the mean and evil Chrissy. She is a hero for putting Chrissy in her place. The problem is that none of what she said was true. She is not a hero. She knows this no matter how hard she is trying to appear as one. She is nothing but a manipulative bully who is attempting to hide her own *fears of abandonment* by sacrificing someone else who is handy. Self-perceived inadequacy precedes guilt. No one can make you feel guilty without your consent. You MUST believe, on some level, that you are responsible for causation in order to accept the verdict of guilty. If an individual can present themselves as a victim, then the guilt perception of those observing will not be directed at the individual, just at the perceived victim. The real victim becomes the target of blame and the initiater becomes the victim and hero simultaneously. This gives the initiater an opportunity to defend their defensive approach, "I'm entitled to get back at Chrissy because I am the victim."

This endeavor to cover fears and exploit the fears and weaknesses of others is a need of some individuals. These people live in a skewed reality where manipulations and deceit become acceptable practice.

They obtain a type of control and self-importance by these deeds. Oftentimes, what is presented to the public (anyone outside of the home) is not what is real.

Example #1

A great example of the superficial belying the real situation is the movie, *The Stepford Wives.*

Example #2

"Let's mow the front yard only. That's all people see."

Example #3

"We cannot afford to buy groceries, but I am going to the club with my buddies tonight and I will pay for everything."

Guilt, deceit, manipulations, threats, hostage-taking, are all behaviors that ensue from repressing the sabotaging fears. If an individual has confronted and contained the fears within, they have no need to attack others. The fears we hold inside often require the sacrifice of others to remain docile. Once addressed, the individual has no need to satiate the fear hunger with attacks on others. The following chapters each address a specific fear. Guidelines for excavations, confrontations, and containment of each will be addressed. It is time you lightened the heavy burden that sabotaging fears have created with you.

Transforming Fears

Many of our fears are born from early experiences we often cannot recall. Even if we have access to those early memories, often the event recalled and the current manifestation of the fear often appear unrelated. Other times, it is easy to see the origination of this emotion. Our goal, in this book, is to assist the reader in identifying the fear type, where/when the fear oriented (the event), what the individual needs to experience in order to overcome the fear, how to put that need experience into action, confront and move past the fear. Although this appears very logical and somewhat simple, it is not. Remember how long ago the fear was instilled; consider how many years that fear has been allowed to lie undisturbed while creating limits to your success. Instant fear control will not happen. It was a process to instill and bury the fear. It is also a process to confront and control it.

As you read through the fears we have included, it is likely that you will see that you are hosting more than one. It is very common to have several fears that feed off of each other, magnifying the damage being done. In this case, each fear must be addressed

Anxiety and Fear

Anxiety presents itself in three ways. The first is cognitively, which occurs through a person's thoughts. This can range from a mild worrying to a severe panic attack. A severe case of anxiety often involves a belief that we are all doomed, preoccupation with the unknown and the dangers presented by this, and even the fear of losing control over one's bladder or bowels. Generalized anxiety disorder also involves fears, albeit they are less severe. These individuals are often focused on financial concerns, the unfairness of life, academic and/or social skills that are lacking, and rejection.

The second presentation of anxiety is behaviorally, which is evidenced by a person's actions. If a person is experiencing anxiety, he or she will avoid situations that may increase these emotions within. When placed in a situation that triggers anxiety, the individual may become disoriented, confused, and try to escape the environment in an urgent manner. At this point, physiological symptoms often appear.

The third way of expressing anxiety is somatically, which is physiological or biological. When an individual is experiencing a panic attack, the body experiences changes: shallow breathing (hyperventilation may occur in extreme cases), dry mouth, cold hands and feet, increased blood pressure, increased perspiration, indigestion and muscle tension. In a more severe panic attack, individuals have reported experiencing what felt like a heart attack. If a situation like this occurs, the individual should be taken to the emergency room immediately.

It is also known that anxiety can serve a positive purpose. It too much time passes between a purposed threat and an individual's reaction to the threat, the individual is placed in a potentially dangerous situation. In this case, anxiety is the emotion that propels us to prepare for a response to a situation. Our basic instinctual response to anxiety is that we can either run or fight. If an individual has no fear, they may become careless and dangerous to themselves and others in not handling situations appropriately.

In 1971, Janis found that moderate anticipatory fear relating to realistic threats is necessary for the development of coping behavior. He believes that individuals with moderate fear levels are more likely to rehears mentally events that were likely to occur and follow. By these rehearsals, the individual has virtually experienced the scary and uncertain situations. The individual is more apt to cope with the fear due to this experience. These functional fears actually serve to protect us from realistic dangers.

People with anxiety do not have a loss of contact with reality. Mild anxiety is present in most individuals. Avoiding situations where one feels inadequate or embarrassed is also quite common. When the anxiety is significant enough to feed off of the sabotaging fears within, it begins to restrict daily activities. Eventually, the individual has become a prisoner of the fear. When anxiety and panic are so significant that they begin to alter your daily life socially, occupationally, even academically, intervention is mandatory.

The self-in-relation theory of psychology ascertains that although men and women can both experience anxiety, women become more anxious when an important relationship is jeopardized. Women tend to find meaning and satisfaction in the preservation of a relationship. This is often related to earlier instance such as parents fighting when the woman was younger. This theory purports that women who remain in an abusive relationship do so because they see themselves as maintaining the relationship regardless of the pain. The woman may even go so far as to request medication to quiet the internal fear of impending abuse.

Elizabeth Ettore (1994) notes that men tend to become anxious due to concerns about work. They "tend to be more focused on their wish for autonomy, mastery, and independence". Due to their need to preserve their sense of identity as the strong individual, they dislike admitting distress, coping difficulties or vulnerability. Therefore, they abuse substances more and seek professional intervention less than women.

Anxiety can come in differing strengths and lengths of duration. Anxiety in a crisis, anxiety as an acute syndrome, or anxiety as a chronic problem is determined by mental health professionals. Most of these are severe enough situations that the individual should consult a physician.

Experiencing anxiety is a normal state. We all become anxious when life offers us uncertainties. There are four basic components to anxiety. Thoughts is the first one. These are normally focused on the identifying issue of concern. An example would be an individual focused on not missing appointments. Working with people who have a history of chronically missed appointments, I have seen this situation grow into one of significant anxiety for some. There are methods we use to address this which will be discussed later in this chapter. When awareness is drawn to a specific situation a person prone to anxiety can quickly escalate. These thoughts can become almost obsessive in nature, even keeping a person up at night.

I have known several therapists who were very focused on financial situations while involved in the financially uncertain arena of private practice. They described experiencing insomnia, hair falling out, even severe attention disintegration due to the anxieties they were experiencing relating to receiving sporadic income. Each of these people eventually left the field of private practice choosing a profession with secure and regulated income. Anxiety happens to us all. The key is to manage it and keep it under control. While not sacrificing goals in the process.

The second component of anxiety is the emotion, and that is fear. Fear and anxiety maintain a parasitic relationship; they feed off of one another. The other emotions present are depression, excitation, interest and discouragement. Anxiety occurs when a threat is made to psychological or physiological well-being of the individual. A fear of abandonment will generate the anxiety of desertion and loneliness. Fear and anxiety require the existence of each other in order to stay strong.

The physical sensation of anxiety is the inner feeling of uneasiness and unrest. Other symptoms can include shortness of breath, dizziness, heart palpitations, sweating, rapid breathing, butterflies in the stomach (a "nervous" stomach), tingling or numbness in the extremities, hot flashes, even chest pain. Motor behavior is the fourth component of anxiety. This is when people fidget. They twirl their hair, chew on a straw, bite their nails, and may experience insomnia.

Generally, professionals agree that anxiety is caused by any or a combination of the following: (1) genetic predisposition, (2) chemicals in the brain, (3) environment, or (4) faulty coping skills.

Men tend to use alcohol and other substances to deal with this anxiety. Women often seek professional intervention from physicians and therapists. It is advisable for all to look to a professional to help with anxiety even in a mild case.

When we are experiencing anxiety, it is easy to respond to others in a negative manner without intending to do harm. Our child begins to repeat one sentence twelve times then moves to different sentence and repeats that one twenty times. If our anxiety level is high, we do not exhibit the tolerance we normally would. When mom and dad are having anxieties about paying bills, and the teenager asks for thirty dollars spending money, the parental response will not be kind. We must focus on self-control, agitation is often the initial response but not the correct one. Professionals can offer direction and guidance so the familial connections are not harmed in the process of containing your anxiety.

Approaches to Lessen One's Anxiety

1. Anxiety Hierarchy

This begins with the individual listing all life events that cause his/ her current anxiety. After creating the list, the individual ranks each in descending order of impact. #1 would be the most anxiety provoking item, #2 would be the second most provoking, etc. until all items have been assigned an intensity value.

Beginning with number one, discuss how this item presents anxiety to the person. Is there any way of eliminating the problem? If it is a person, is there any way of putting distance between the individual and the problem person? After proximity is determined, the focus is de-powering the item. If the item defined is finances, and the problem is that there are too many bills and not enough money, the obvious solution is to change the power distribution. Bills and money must, at the very least, be equal. Preferably, money would be the heavier power.

Problem solve this situation by brainstorming with the person on how to increase the money flow:

- Can anyone in the home get an additional job for extra income?

- Is anyone in the home talented in the manner of crafts, cooking, mechanics, day care, cleaning or perhaps art? These are ways to earn extra cash.

- Is it possible to consolidate the bills by utilizing a loan?

- Have all bank options (such as loans) been explored?

- Is it possible to have a yard sale or directly sell high dollar play toys like motorcycles or hobby cars?

Develop a plan to address the first anxiety. This plan should contain short term goals that can be done immediately and should show results within three weeks maximum. Construct long term goals that are extensions of the short term goals that should show results in 6-12 months. The final goal is what we stated in the beginning, to decrease the money outgo and increase the money in.

When a person is experiencing anxiety, the problem solving skills, even when normally good, become inadequate. The person is often experiencing an avalanche sensation. They feel as if they are smothering and trying to gasp for air. No matter how hard they struggle, they cannot get out from under the layers of snow (anxiety provoking life situations). At these times, they need another person to shovel them out. Each item on the hierarchy is addressed in the same manner: how it presents, problem solve solutions and develop short and long term goals.

2. Desensitization

Developed originally by Mary Cover Jones in the 1950's, this can be used to eventually confront and contain anxiety. Simplifying her therapeutic approach of pairing a positive with a negative, we will pair a pleasing stimuli with the one causing the anxiety emotion.

Let's consider Jack and his anxiety provoking trigger: Monday morning. Jack is not happy in his job, but enjoys his occupation. He is a coach at a local junior high. Although he would rather be coaching at a college, he is aware that he is responsible for supporting his family, so he routinely arrives at the junior high to impart his infallible wisdom and talent on seventh and eighth graders. Each Sunday evening, Jack becomes nauseous and develops a severe migraine. He cannot sleep well; he tosses and turns. He gets out of bed every two to three hours to use the bathroom even though he really doesn't need to. Monday mornings he is wide awake an hour before the alarm sounds, dreading his trip to work. He is irritable to his family and coworkers. His students avoid him.

In this approach, we would first identify why Jack dreads only Mondays when he works each day. Jack maintains that Monday signifies another week wasted at doing what he doesn't like to do. If he can make it through Monday, the rest of the week is downhill.

We want to address Monday mornings as the identified problem. If Monday is not so dreaded, Sunday nights become more pleasant as well since they precipitate Mondays.
Jack loves coffee. He derives great pleasure from gourmet coffee and special pastries.

Perhaps, each Monday morning, Jack's wife can "surprise" him with goodies from the local coffee shop. He is now given a large latte' and two gooey, custard filled pastries. This gives him something to look forward to. It would be an added bonus if Jack allowed himself to go out for lunch each Monday. Even though he normally brings his lunch or eats the cafeteria food, this is now a special occasion. It's Monday! Treat yourself!

As simple as this sounds, it is very effective. Additions could always improve the situation. Perhaps a shoulder massage on Sunday afternoons would decrease his impending tension. Renting a movie on Sunday night can take away the dreading feeling of the rapidly approaching Monday. Jack also needs to become proactive in his career. He must begin to prepare himself for his occupational goal of college coaching. What are the steps he must master in order to achieve that goal? He should map out his strategies and begin.

3. Relaxation Techniques

Both of our situations above could benefit from adding this element into their routine. There are many techniques available. The goal is to teach a person to achieve relaxation in a calm situation and eventually generalize that ability for use in an anxiety provoking situation. I am going to address a specific combination of techniques I use with clients.

Step 1.

Remove shoes and any restrictive adornments such as belts or scarves. Sit straight in a chair with arms at sides. Your legs should be at a 45 degree angle to your sitting body. Clinch both hands until the knuckles of your fists are white. While doing this, hold your breath. Clinch and hold breath for twenty to thirty seconds. Exhale. Repeat five times.

Step 2.

Stand up. Bend your knees and shuffle feet, walking in this position for five minutes. The muscles in your lower torso should be tight. Focus on navel as center of gravity.

Step 3.

Lie down on your back, arms at your side. The room should be dark or shadowed. A white noise maker should be running for consistency.

Step 4

A progressive relaxation technique is done. Each body part is address and told to relax, from toe to head.

Step 5

Guided imagery is performed. There are a number of these available.

Step 6

After the procedure has concluded, the person is asked to stand up and do stretching exercises.

Step 7

Process and discuss the events.

There are a number of programs available that you can use. I use the recoding I made that addresses the progressive relaxation and guided imagery journey (see resources on page___ to order). Routinely, people will comment about the journey, how they felt cold at some points, so snug and safe at other points. After working on this several times with a client, the client is able to do the process themselves. That is the goal of relaxation, for the person to be able to implement it when they need it.

4. Problem Solving and Goal Setting

This is the same procedure discussed earlier (anxiety hierarchy) except the hierarchy is not used. The individual may just need to express worries and concerns to someone who is not a therapist. Sometimes an objective observer can put anxieties into perspective.

An example of this is as follows:

Wilma is concerned that her husband doesn't find her attractive anymore. She is forty-five and somewhat overweight. She feels ugly, heavy, and uninteresting. When he begins working late three nights a week, this only reinforces her anxieties. She waits for him at home, pacing the floor, allowing herself to obsess about him being with another woman who looks beautiful and is fascinating.

Putting these thoughts in perspective is what Wilma needs help doing. Validation that the husband is really at work would help. Showing concrete proof,such as a time sheet, would encourage Wilma's trust. Addressing her displeasure with her appearance and life also needs to happen. At this point, a list of what changes she wants to make and how to make them is prudent. Set the short term and long term goals. Help her obtain information regarding furthering her education or professional skills.

5. Journaling

The use of narration in therapy is very effective. I have used different versions of journaling to address the specific needs of my clients. Basically, a journal can have any theme it needs. The journal should be private to all except the author. It is the author's option when and if to share it. In therapy, the client will share portions (or all) with the therapist which relate to a specific goal.

I have used the journal as a poetry collection working with teen females exhibiting depression and a positive writing ability, they write their poems. We discuss the poems in regard to what their current life experiences are, how they are being regarded, and how the person is dealing with life stress. The poetry will show the mood of the writer as well as the intent. Writing is a catharsis, a release. The writer often reports feeling relief after the journal entry or poem is completed.

The journal is handy as an anger outlet. When working with someone who has difficulty containing the anger, I have the client journal each event, each day, that generates the anger feelings. I have them describe, in extreme detail, how the emotion began, how it grew, when they knew they were consumed by it, and what they did to remove themselves from the situation. Each entry is dated. I also suggest they write any emotions that are strong:

Example:

I HATE YOU MRS. SMITH

This was directed at a teacher by one of my clients in her journal. I also need to say that in the past she would have told the teacher this verbally and in an aggressive tone. Now she writes it, in all capital letters and with a lot of pressure, in her journal. This journal helps us monitor the anger and how it changes.

Also useful is the memory journal. When a person is having traumatic memories regarding specific situations of abuse or neglect, this is very appropriate. The memories should be written without regard to punctuation or spelling. It should be a complete stream of consciousness. Once the memories are logged, the person often feels a sort of exhaustion. Processing the journal later with a trained therapist is advisable.

Then there is always the dreamer's notebook. Psychology has a rich history of dream analysis. Transcribing one's dreams to analyze at a later date is useful. Keeping the dreamer's notebook beside one's bed, so the dream can be logged immediately upon awakening, is advised. Keep a writing utensil there as well. Many books are available to assist you in the analysis. Remember that we often dream in symbols, not literal translations.

I have also used the journaling approach in a diary format. I will encourage clients to summarize their day on a daily basis. Write down what went right and what you would like to change. We address these thoughts in session. I know someone who keeps an ongoing narrative of her husband's comments to her. She believes he is the cause of her anxiety and is trying to see how many positive comments he makes per week. Currently his negative comments outnumber the positive.

6. Exaggeration

This encourages the person to exaggerate the bad effects he/she is afraid might happen as a result of an action. Theoretically, this exaggeration decreases the anxiety which is resulting from the unknown.

For example:

Jill wants to call Tom and ask him out on a date. She is afraid of rejection. This approach suggests that Jill exaggerate the possible negative outcome.

"If I call him, he will laugh at me and tell everyone he rejected me."

The point in this approach involves the probability that the person exaggerating will realize the world does not end if the telephone call turns out negatively. This can work because the person has gradually decided to keep control over the exaggerated emotions by realizing these emotions were not based on a real danger.

7. Cognitive restructuring

Positive self-talk is very effective. Negative self-talk is very effective. Many of us are eager to criticize our actions but do not encourage our actions. It is common to hear people refer to themselves in derogatory terms (loser, stupid, idiot) when they fail at something. But what if that same person said, "Good job trying. That shows bravery and intellect just to attempt what you did. Way to go"? Wouldn't that be more encouraging?

We will talk about this in more detail in a later chapter. Cognitive restructuring is one of the easiest and most difficult intervention available. People are so eager to discount anything that is simple. This is powerful.

If a person has test anxiety, what are they really afraid of? Parental displeasure? Failing the class? At this point, the individual has already visualized themselves failing a test they have not read. The person is convincing the self that something bad is inevitable. It is a no win situation. To reduce this fear, say something positive, "Even if I fail the test, I will not become a bad person. This test is not an indicator of my self-worth. It is just a test." I have seen inadequate therapists pass licensing exams and brilliant practitioners fail them. A test is not a measure of character nor interactive abilities. It measures book knowledge and/or test taking skills

We will also discuss visualization in a later chapter. Visualization goes hand-in-hand with cognitive restructuring. Part of an athlete's training is to visualize the end of the race. They see themselves crossing the finish line successfully. The athlete will focus on the mental vision of running, keeping time, even breathing in time. This is very powerful. Subconsciously, we must be aware that we can win. Perceived self-defeat is an antithesis to success. You can still act on a positive thought and optimism even if you are afraid. This is how fear and anxiety are contained. It is also worth noting that athletes are instructed to prepare properly for each contest noting that each is different in some way. A complete preparation is required they complete. You should prepare for each exam as well. Rest, eat well, and know what the exam will require to make this endeavor a success.

8. Gradual exposure

Gradually exposing yourself to the object of anxiety or fear is another option. Before employing this approach, I would suggest using the anxiety hierarchy, desensitization, and cognitive restructuring. Gradual exposure to feared stimuli should always be experienced with a safety person for maximum success. The person is a security..

A safety person is someone you trust for safety. Using this approach, the individual encounters the anxiety producing item from far away, then gets closer each time. Obviously, if the object can do one harm, it is best NOT to employ this technique. The person experiencing an anxiety to this item sees It as dangerous on some level. Even if the item cannot actually do harm, perceived harm is also dangerous.

Example:

Linda is experiences anxiety when she is around a large group of people. Using this approach, she would be introduced to gradually larger groups of people as she became comfortable with the smaller groups.

Using this approach, Linda would be taken to a grocery store in off peak hours. She would be given a grocery list to focus on. Her safety person would accompany her. In order to complete the assignment successfully, she must put each item on the list in her basket and make it through the check out cashier. This must be done with the minimal amount of anxiety symptoms. Each time she visits the grocery store, the crowds would be larger, gradually working up to shopping during peak hours in large crowds. She can also make "homework" trips to the restaurants at differing times of crowdedness to monitor her maximum level of exposure she can handle with low anxiety.

She must be accompanied by the safety person. If not, the symptoms of anxiety could present and she would be alone and vulnerable. This way, someone else is there to help her refocus and utilize relaxation techniques when needed.

Remember that you control your anxieties and fears. They cannot control you. Past experiences may have left you afraid or scarred. These experiences must be allowed to remain in the past. It is very possible for the mind to receive cues from the imagination regarding possible future occurrences which are connected to your fears. This will increase the anxiety. In reality, we only have control over ourselves. As hard as we may try, we cannot completely control our children, spouse, co-workers, boss, or economy. We can only make the self do what we want. Realizing this is imperative when establishing limits to responsibility. Knowing what one needs to feel safe is also necessary.

To be safe, we must understand our fear. Explore the causation of the fear and how it has been well fed all of these years. Most of the time, confusion surrounds fear because we seem to lose our objectivity when confronting it. Realize that you have limits in dealing with this fear. Those limits may change as you develop more coping strategies and options. Perhaps the fear must be contained at this time and confronted at the later time.

There are five keys to confronting fear:

- Define the fear

- Discover the origin of the fear

- Explore why you fear the item so intensely

- Acknowledge and accept that the fear does exist

- Face the fear and control it

You may never completely eradicate the fear or anxiety. The goal is to learn to take charge of these and determine just how powerful you will allow the anxiety to be. Anxiety does not need to control your life plans. You can live a life to the fullest, with complete happiness if the fear and anxiety are contained. Fears are self-sabotaging. No matter how you try to disguise them, they end up destroying what you want from life. Part of fear is feeling out of control. Taking control can cause other problems, however; fear can be the result of trying to control too much. You must take this power away from them and be in control. Minimize their impact and effect upon you. They will try to resurface occasionally, but with the tools you have, you can control them.

To avoid being controlled and immobilized by fear, you must realize that fear helps us focus attention on an immediate threat. It is important to detach yourself from the situation and remain clear-headed. You must be cognizant enough to plan your next move. Determine if there is a valid reason, an objective reason, for your anxiety. Taking action is important. These actions should not be emotionally based. Just because you are angry at someone, the solution reaction is not to hit them. Hitting them is an emotional reaction. Your appropriate solution reaction should be one that would improve your standing and security in the situation.

Isaac Marks, in *Living with Fear*, identifies five truths regarding anxiety:

- Anxiety is unpleasant but rarely dangerous

- You should avoid escape

- You should face the fear

- The longer you face anxiety, the better

- The more rapidly you confront the world, the more quickly your fear will fade

Change is difficult. In order to address these anxieties and fears, you must be interested in doing so. Once interested, you must have the motivation to make the change occur. Motivation may not be constant. In order for a full change to occur in your life, you must manage the motivation to be at an effective level. It is easy to make yourself a promise to improve your life style or rid yourself of anxiety based on a personal tragedy such as death of a loved one or a family crisis. It is harder to maintain that focus after the process begins. Controlling fears is challenging and difficult. We tend to avoid such things that do not come easily. Discouragement is likely. Keep focused and keep on task.

What are some commonly negative ways to handle fears? Deny it. People who are in denial of fear appear as martyrs, righteous and pious, mired in self-pity and guilt. Perhaps an individual will discount the fear as being minimal and insignificant. These people often are pessimistic, depressed, even cynical. They turn to addictions and tend to be cold and passionless. Someone may become defensive and attack anyone who may suggest they have fear. These people experience self-hate and self-ridicule. Avoidance of the feared item is another way of (negatively) handling fears. This would be the bully type of person, at school or at the office. The last one Is refusal. A person refused the address the fear and becomes involved in dangerous pursuits to prove they are not afraid of anything, such as sky-diving or extreme sports.

Fear, uncertainty and doubt combine to create anxiety. John Moore (2005) maintains that these can be dealt with by (1) imaging yourself meeting your goals, (2) tuning out negative remarks by others, (3) avoiding negative self-talk, and (4) surrounding yourself with positive people who have a similar goal. Mr. Moore utilizes the positivity from without and within as tools for focusing and motivating.

Destructive patterns of behavior not only include substance addictions, they include anxiety and fear. These are counterproductive to success. We all have some levels of insecurities which are based on early childhood trauma, misunderstandings, and loss. We are creatures of habit and begin responding to similar situations in the same way. When presented with a familiar dilemma, the individual must not immediately respond in the same destructive manner. Since insecurities create vulnerabilities, the individual is frantically attempting to create a wall of protection as he/she always has. This wall is faulty and not well constructed. It needs to be knocked down. In order to change our responses, we must be able to change the way we perceive situations.

The first step is to analyze exactly how you are perceiving the situation. Are you accepting responsibility and ownership for your thoughts and feelings? No one can make you feel any way you do not agree to feel. Whenever you catch yourself giving power to someone else, you must stop, "She made me feel insignificant," is inaccurate. The truth is that she said something that you allowed to hurt your feelings. Now you are upset and blaming this person because you allowed yourself to do so. No one is to blame for your feelings except you. If it hurts, either don't let it in or change it.

You do not have to accept any faulty reasoning. When the negative self-talk begins, use a strategy to stop it. Make it positive. You cannot control life, you cannot control others, but you can control yourself and your responses to life and others. Trust yourself to be secure. Maintain your motivation and focus. Now is the best time to begin this new approach to ridding yourself of the self-sabotaging fears that interfere with your life goals and aspirations.

Fear of Failure

"There is no need to try. I'd only fail."

"Why would that store want to hire me? It's a waste of my time to apply."

"I cannot go to college. I'm not smart enough."

"Why should I even go out on a date? My relationships don't work out."

The fear of failure is defined as someone neglecting to follow through on a task because the individual is convinced failure in imminent. The individual often cites numerous situations from the past to support the "do not try" theory. Justification is attempted. The person attempts to justify to others that they are too tired, too put upon, perennially unlucky, perhaps even undeserving. The person attempts to justify these thoughts by reminding others of past failures. The illogic here is just because the past contains failures doesn't mean the future will as well. Statistically, with numerous failures, the person is due at least one future success.

Excuses are cheap. They are not to be confused with reasons. It is always harder to try than to give up. This individual must not be allowed to give excuses. Family and friends, the support system, only enables and encourages the individual not to try something new when they accept these flimsy overused excuses.

Acknowledge the individual's past. The person who experiences fear of failure often has some pretty intense history. The history usually involves being an overachiever. The overachiever is always working so hard as not to have any mistakes that may constitute what he/she perceives as failure. Understand that this person's definition of failure may be quite different than that of others. In fact, everyone has his or her own definition of failure.

Many overachievers tie their self-worth to their accomplishments. They are terrified of the possible confirmation that they are not superior. Many of these individuals excelled in academics. The person would believe failure if his/her test score was below an "A". This person would routinely run himself or herself physically to the ground in order to surpass the set office quota for sales or performance. If this individual scored an "average" on a work or academic evaluation, that score becomes their self-assessment and what they perceive their peers believe them to be. This person works too many hours and often exhibits "control issues".

Being in control of events is one way to make sure the work is done and done well. This individual is likely to delegate very little, preferring to complete the project alone or with little intervention. Once again, if the project fails, the person sees it as a direct reflection on him/her. Unfortunately for the coworkers, this often results in barked orders and hurt feelings. Coworkers wonder if the individual doesn't trust them enough to involve them in the project. These individuals are not mean or selfish people. They are very performance driven and make great executives. The trick is not to alienate everyone else along the way. Truthfully, if one person can do a great job on a project, imagine the production quality of three individuals on the same project with each giving 100%.

This individual has a fear of failure. They are an overachiever and demanding. The next question is regarding the motivation level. Someone with the fear of failure may be so totally incapacitated by this fear that they are too terrified to try anything. The individual chooses not to be the overachiever. This individual is terrified of even trying to go to school. This individual would briefly consider attending school, and then be too afraid of encountering the registration process. They would be convinced of certain inability in completing the process. This individual would not try to study to impress her and others. This person would give up before beginning. This individual would be likely to drop out of the public school system at an early age, perhaps high school. The fear can become so encompassing that the person's vision of impending failure outweighs any opportunity of trying for success.

Addressing the Needs

We have two completely different responses to this one fear. Let's look at what each individual's true needs are. Person #1 needs: acceptance, validation, support from coworkers, reassurance that others will not let her/him down, relaxation strategies, self-esteem building, and social skills training.

Person #1 needs acceptance from the peer group at work. Since this person is bordering workaholic status due to the need for overachieving, approval and appreciation from the coworkers shows acknowledgement of efforts. When they give validation through verbal praise, the individual feels the effort expended was worth it. Without this validation, the overachiever can easily adopt a martyr persona. The martyr is someone who feels they give and give and give of themselves, but no one appreciates it. The martyr often believes he/she is doing the majority, if not all, of the work and is routinely taken for granted. Once an individual has adopted the martyr stance, productivity declines due to this thought pattern. When an overachiever becomes bitter and disgruntled, work performance plummets. These people need persistent acknowledgement.

Support from coworkers creates a bond between the individual and peers. This individual is likely to have a very small, if any, social life. The person puts all of the energy and availability into the chosen profession. When peers voice concern about the carnival's family, health, even general conversation, this is appreciated deeply. Once the person feels connected to others at work, a trust can begin. This person needs to learn to work with others. Teamwork is not only about sharing responsibility. It is about improving social skills, learning to share as adults. Teamwork should be encouraged for this person. It will be very difficult at first for the individual to "let go" enough to allow others a chance to prove their sincere intentions. This person will not tolerate mistakes very well. If at all possible, someone else should organize the team project, involving this individual, so with careful monitoring, no mistakes are made. At this early stage, involving one in a group project that tanks due to lack of organization and effort is detrimental to further development. This person is trying to redevelop a level of trust of others and self. Set backs still result in the same negative self-talk we opened the chapter with. This person will add the event to their list of illogical justifications.

Person #2 needs: motivation, support, guidance, focus, and a game plan. Until this individual can garner the above needs, he/she is unable to move forward. At this point, we really just want to nudge the person to make a move. We need them to show some momentum. This person is hiding in the fear. The fear itself is the rationalization for doing nothing. She has perceived helplessness and inadequacies.

The person rationalizes, "If I try to register for classes, I'll just get lost." This grows, the negativity feeding on itself. "I'll become so confused, I won't know where to go. I'll be a failure again and everyone will laugh at me. It's better for me to just stay home and not even try."

Establishing a powerful support system for this individual is a must. The support system will need to encourage, perhaps even go as far as to drive this person to a location to perform a task. Responsibility training is necessary. This individual will be content to live in the fear bubble, allowing others to think for them, wait on them, and take care of them. Eventually, the individual develops a learned helplessness that overpowers the fear. This person can become a self-imposed invalid with help from well-meaning family and friends. It is imperative that a list of responsibilities be drafted.

This person should be held accountable for household chores. This person should be urged strongly to venture outside of the fear zone. For example, let's say that Sarah's fear of failure has grown to the degree she refused to go grocery shopping because she is convinced that she will buy the wrong items and upset the family. Her family, in an effort to not provoke anxiety and distress, has allowed Sarah to make these excused for years. At this time, Sarah needs to work her way up to grocery shopping as one of her chores/responsibilities. It would be a great idea to begin this providing a list of items previously agreed upon to purchase, and another family member, whom Sarah feels safe around, to accompany her. It is a good idea to make this outing during the week, during the day when the store is somewhat empty. If Sarah is experiencing anxiety related to shopping, it is not a good idea to put her in a situation of overcrowding and loud noises.

The first trip should be very brief. As the visits increase, so can the length of time spent at the store.

This one example of grocery shopping addresses the needs attributed to person #2. The person is required to confront the situation she connected to the fear. In this confrontation, the situation was arranged so that success was imminent. The person feels success for the first time in a long while. The best way to overcome failure is through repeated success. Her support system has proven their loyalty to her by accompaniment. The support system has reassured the success of the individual. The person feels loved, safe and secure.

Origins of Fear of Failure

Addressing the individual's needs is a productive manner to containing the fear and its symptoms. After the fear is immobilized, it needs to readdressed and confronted. This occurs when we explore the origin of the fear. When did the individual develop this fear? What events precipitated the birth of the fear?

I have found it very helpful to utilize the parent/child approach in this phase of fear eradication. Framo (1982) developed a psychological theory called Object Relations. In this theory, individuals play roles. The theory is fascinating in the sense that the individual can be taught to switch roles. The two roles I focus on when approaching a fear situation is the Parent and the Child. Framo used this approach in the family therapy setting as well.

When working with an adult who is containing the fear, I listen to their description of the fear. I ask them to describe it with human characteristics. I refer to the Fear as a proper noun. When a traumatic situation has occurred in one's early life and has let the person a hostage within himself or herself, this Fear takes on the personage of a Jailer. I urge the person to tell this Jailer the damage that has been caused through this hostage situation.

We then begin our journey back through time, the individual speaking as an Adult viewing the younger years. When the person identifies the situation that gave birth to the fear, oftentimes the role changes to that of Child. The description of events is most often through the eyes of the child, at the age it was initially experienced. After the disclosure has ended, the reestablishment of the individual in the Adult role is necessary.

However, addressing the issue is most effective when done through the Child who experienced it. The Child needs to be able to grieve, cry, become angry, whatever needs to be experienced in order to move on. The adult can then adopt the anger, which was never afforded to the Child. The Adult can then deal with the fear on a different level and easily win. What defeats the Child doesn't defeat the Adult.

Let's explore some of the more common origins of the fear of failure.

Home environment:

*Parents may have high standards; it may be difficult for the child to meet these expectations.

*Parents may be very successful and the child feels inferior in ability and performance.

*Parents may be sacrificing heavily to invest in the child's education and activities. The child feels he/she "owes" the parents a tremendous debt.

*Parents may be overly critical of child's performance. The parent may be hard to satisfy. Compliments and reassurances are few.

*Child may not receive as much attention as he/she requires. Being superior in all aspects may be the way approval and attention is received.

*Limits and boundaries were too lax or too strict.

Academic environment:

*Student realizes from an early age that if she is "the smartest" in class, then teachers and peers acknowledge that; student equates attention with respect, friends, and acceptance

*Student may have a learning disability that makes it difficult to perform. Student becomes used to low grades, perceived teacher disapproval and begins to act out negatively to compensate for the lack of positive attention. A "class clown" is created.

Personality Self-Sabotage:

*Low self-esteem (feelings of inadequacies)
*Demanding
*Bullying
*Aggressive and potentially hostile
*Frustrated
*Controlling
*Achievement orientation to one extreme (overachiever or nonachiever)
*Feels rejected easily
*Can overlap with fear of abandonment

When a person has fear of failure, they are in constant need of reassurances. They tend toward criticism of self. This person is likely to be overheard chastising him or herself for a simple mistake.

"Jeeze, how stupid, stupid, stupid…".

The individual is quick to perceive criticism form others as well. This individual is usually quite sensitive. The feelings are hurt easily. When a coworker makes a comment that may be taken negatively, it WILL be. Many times, the person is responding to a perceived tone or insinuation, not the actual word choice. When we do this, it is due to our feelings of inadequacies and inferiority. We believe we are not as proficient as we should be. When one has a fear of failure, he/she often believes, in the deepest core of the being, that he/she is not worthy of the job (they) are doing and eventually someone will discover this horrible truth.

When someone has a fear of failure, he/she is terrified at not following through on something that should be. For example, a marriage. Fear of failure can motivate an individual to stay in an abusive marriage because,"If this marriage fails, I fail." Illogical thought permeates the mindset of fear. Even though the individual is beaten and terrified, the illogic is strong. When the abuser is aware of this fear, it is easily exploited.

"What? You are going to leave me? Leave this marriage? You go ahead and run back to your mom. Show her she's always been right about you. You *can't* do anything right. You are such a failure."

The respondent is left in a no-win situation. The fear will not allow the ending of the marriage. The marriage is perceived as another commitment. The partner is acutely aware of this fear and parlays it into a weakness. The only way to win this situation is to establish success. Success **always** overcomes failure. Success comes in the form of increase self-esteem and independence. When an individual has a strong sense of self, that sense will not allow the self to be abused. In the case of our abused individual, the best way to assist her is in building empowerment.

Many books are written covering pillars of self-esteem and creating an empowered individual. If someone is being abused, they need to find safety immediately. Therapy is a good way to confront and overcome the factors leading to and resulting from an abusive relationship.

A fear of failure, seated early in one's life, is commonly evolved from a trauma associated with no acceptance by peers. When a child is ridiculed and treated as an outcast, the child wants desperately to fit in. The child realizes that as an adult, if they put in more effort and more time, they become the individual others look up to. As an adult they receive the attention and acceptance they craved as a child. In accordance with this theory, if failure were ever an option, the individual would become convinced they would lose the respect and stature they have achieved through hard work and diligence. The fear of the past overlaps this fear of failure.

Fear of the Past

"If I save 80% of my income, living frugally, I will never know poverty again."

"If I can prove myself occupationally, I will earn the respect I have always deserved but have been denied."

"If I never become involved in a serious relationship, no one can hurt me again."

"Stop yelling at me! When you do, I see and hear my father."

The fear of the past repeating itself is a substantial load to carry. This often involves guilt on some level. The individual often feels they were responsible for a family member's action years earlier. It is common for the adult to sustain the belief, albeit subconsciously, that he/she was actually responsible for her parents divorce. Adults often say very hurtful things in the heat of severe discord. It is possible that in the heat of the moment, the parent (s) suggested the child was to blame for the split.

"If you weren't so much trouble, your father would have stayed."

"You're always needing something. You are too expensive."

These comments were made out of frustration and anger. Human nature looks to blame someone else for the disaster because it is much less painful than looking inward and accepting self-blame. In the event there is no one to directly assign blame to, it is convenient to identify a scapegoat. A scapegoat is created when a family member, usually a parent, projects his/her emotions on the child. The scapegoat is the one most strongly connected to the family. According to Bowen (1976), children can represent valued or feared expectations to the parents. Roles are assigned to the child on the basis of the parent (s) unresolved needs. Unable to tolerate responsibility for a failed relationship, the adult projects that responsibility on the child, verbally blaming the child. Being an impressionable child, the individual carries the responsibility of failure into adulthood. As an adult, the person desperately attempts to avoid making the same mistake again. It is possible the individual will not remember the earlier accusations made by the parents or even specific events, but is aware of the firm stance he currently takes to avoid a potentially similar catastrophe.

Example 1

In the event of divorce or separation, the child should be involved in the communication process to a degree. The child should always be reassured he/she had no role in the split. Accessibility to both parents (as long as no criminal behavior was involved) should be made. Negative verbalizations and accusations from one parent about the other should not be allowed. This places the child in the middle of a potential conflict. A tug of was ensures. When a child matures with the perceived burden of responsibility of parental divorce, the entire social strata of his/her life is altered. Loneliness becomes preferable to the belief of certain failure in the event of an interpersonal relationship. The person sabotages any romantic relationships before the significant other can leave. The illogic emanating from the fear focuses on:

- "I am unlovable. I ruin relationships."

- "I am unworthy of sustaining a positive relationship."

- "Why would I become involved with someone I care about, only to destroy his/her life with my certain failure in relationships?"

Let's look at a different scenario that can be based on fear of the past repeating itself. When a child is raised in an environment short on finances, he often desires materialistic items that are too expensive. This is a normal response. When the child is unable to procure these items, one of two things happens. The child either accepts the limits of the household or doesn't. If limits are accepted, the child learns to succeed within those set limits. This individual often aspires to success. Using the memory of having few materialistic items can be a motivator for many things: education, security, humanitarianism, altruism, even relationships.

The individual who becomes angry at the earlier materialistic restrictions can also use the anger as a motivator. The anger motivates one to succeed regardless of whom they must step on or over. The success becomes the goal. Happiness, fulfillment, satisfaction, helping others, even involvement in a healthy relationship is not seen as important goals. These people focus solely on the prize of success and material items. They are often ruthless and self-centered.

Carl Jung (1939) coined a phrase, inferiority complex, that describes an individual who suffered through adversity as a child and, as an adult, is determined to make others pay for his/her past pain. Once again, the Child inside the Adult, has not confronted the pain and is still looking for revenge. An example of this would be the following:

Example 2

When Bert was a young boy, he was skinny, gangly, and wore thick glasses. The other children made fun of him. He tried to become a scholar in order to make friends and receive positive attention.

Academics were not his strong suit. Always alone, he developed an intense hatred for the "popular" kids. College wasn't any more pleasant. Others ridiculed him since his major was kinesthetics. He wanted to be a coach. Many disparaging remarks regarding his mental acuity were made. Once he graduated, his main goal was revenge. Eventually Bert became a Production Manager in an assembly plant. He was a tyrant. He ridiculed, harassed, gossiped, and was relentless to those he supervised. Subconsciously, Bert was making them pay for his tormented past.

Needs

Obviously, Bert was miserable. Revenge never makes the pain go away. It is a hunger that is seldom satisfied. Revenge is not the solution to dissolving a fear of the past. Let's look at the needs held by each of these main characters. The child in scenario #1 was blamed for the parental separation. As an adult, he is unable to maintain a relationship due to the fear of destroying someone he loves. His needs: to be absolved of the blame placed on him by the parent, goal setting, a strategy plan of how to achieve the goals, and self-confidence.

The Adult needs to forgive the Child. As a man, this individual must allow himself to return to the origination of the fear. He needs to be able to go back to the days he chose to accept this blame. He must address the illogic that the parent used while blaming him. Verbally addressing the illogic is done by stating the message he as a child, received from the parent:

"I recall mother saying that Dad left because I demanded too much of her time. I was too high maintenance. My toys and clothes were too expensive. He ran away from me. When he left me, he left her."

In addressing this, the Adult is challenged to explore the missing pieces. Does he remember his parents arguing? What about? Was there anything ever said, to the boy, by the father, that would support this "high maintenance" theory? Had Dad left before? Where is Dad now? Has he remarried? The point of this is to help the Child understand that when parents split up they do it because *they* cannot make the marriage work. Even if the child was peripherally involved in the split, it was still a decision made between two adults and was the total responsibility of these two adults. If an adult really dissolves a marriage because a child is costly, then the adult needs some individual interventions. Even if this was a true statement, the child is still *not* to blame. The parent has not met his/her responsibilities to the child.

An exploration of excuses and reasons must be explored as mentioned in an earlier chapter. A reason has a logical, substantial, objective and provable base. An excuse is something plausible that gets an individual "off of the hook". An excuse is often skewed and manipulated to serve the purpose of absolution.

The Child is then challenged with the memories he has identified. Which are viable? Which are excuses? The Adult is then given the same challenge. The difficult part of this exercise is to watch the Adult process the understanding that all of these past years have been spent nursing his father's excuses. He has put his father's flimsy excuses before his own happiness and fulfillment. His father wanted out of the marriage. His mother wasn't ready to take responsibility for the split and neither was Dad. The boy was used as a scapegoat from an early age. He accepted the burden and the guilt given to him by two adults who should never had involved him in this manner. Now, the child has become an adult and must reevaluate his parents, decisions on the level of adult-to-adult.

Guilt is a major player in this process. Responsibility can be connected to guilt. Deep seated guilt and self-loathing can occur when a person, regardless of age, feels he/she has not responded adequately in a situation that has hurt someone he/she cared about.

An individual living with a self-perceived responsibility failure is prone to control-seeking behavior (Charlton, 1996). The person reasons that if they can be in control of situations, they can protect their present from the past. Perhaps the past need never repeat itself if the situation can be managed/ controlled. This overlaps with *fear of failure* characteristics.

The Adult must address the guilt of the Child. The Adult within needs to forgive the child, releasing him from the responsibility of keeping his parents together. The Adult must then look at his own life, exploring his need for control.

Goal setting and a strategy for obtaining each goal are needed. This Adult has just shed a huge burden, which has prevented him from meaningful relationships that do not need to end. The Adult has to allow himself permission to build his present and future the way he desire but is afraid to. He is no longer shackled by a fear of the past because he is aware he had no responsibility in the divorce. Goal setting should contain both short-term goals and long-term goals.

Short-term goals are attainable within one to six months. Long-term goals are accomplished within six months to a year. Long-term goals are the stepping-stones needed to acquire the overall goal. Short term goals may include an increased social life, re-establishing contact with old friends (male and female), trying to become more patient and calm concerning relationship and work issues, even increasing communication with the parents. These stepping stones should directly lead to the long term goals which are more significant: begin dating more seriously (allowing self to believe there can be a future with this person), exploring old relationships that may have extinguished due to the individual's inability to follow through with it, learning to trust others, approaching the parent-child relationship on a new level. The ultimate goal would be one of happiness and freedom from fear. The best way to combat a fear of the past is to establish a promising future, believe in its possibilities, and become dedicated to achieving your goals.

In Example #2, our first subject is raised in a non-materialistic environment. Finances are tight and strained. In the first scenario, the individual chooses to work within the limits set. The need is to sustain the ability to use positive thinking and cognitive restructuring. Goal setting for future accomplishments is also important. This person employs the positive thinking approach that focuses on eventual total success while enforcing present encouragement. The present encouragement is still a type of success. This encouragement focuses on finding the positives in the current environment. Attempt not to focus or consider the negative aspects. Adults who have survived impoverished early years often don't remember the bitter negatives. In recollections, they speak of the tightness and safety of the family unit. "We didn't know we were poor. We always had shelter and plenty to eat."

Those who do remember the bitterly cold winters, the nights they went to bed hungry due to lack of food in the house, do not often do so with bitterness. It is more of a solid resolution of the way things used to be and cannot be changed. It is a possibility that these memories can be restructured to make one motivated and more compassionate toward others.

Cognitive restructuring is a therapeutic tool used with great success. This is taking a negative situation, finding the positive aspects of it, and then flipping the situation to a positive bent. If an individual is able to view an unpleasant situation positively, it decreases the anxiety, stress, depression and anger, which often accompany such events.

Here are examples of cognitive restructuring:

Example #1

Adolescent: "My mother is so nosy. She wants to know where I am, who I am with, when I'll be home. She needs to get off of my back!"

Restructuring Statement: "Your mother cares so much about you that she wants you to be safe. Can you call her to let her know where you can be reached in case of an emergency?"

Example #2

Husband: "My wife nags me all the time. No matter what I do it's never enough. She even tells me how to dress, as if I were a child."

Restructuring Statement: "Your wife is trying to help you. She thinks she is giving you helpful advise that will assist you in your career. It's only because she loves you so much that she notices everything you do and don't do. She gives you a lot of attention."

Goal setting is important in this situation as well. Cognitive restructuring is a great tool to get through the immediate situation. One must have a plan of eventual success as well. This individual must know where he/she is headed, and know how to get to this ultimate goal. This is a road map needed for survival. Used in tandem with the positive thinking approach and cognitive restructuring, the person also knows where he/she is directed. The light at the end of the tunnel is very significant. If we become mired in the present, seeing no way out, then we lose our momentum. We become dead weight, sinking in our own despair. Goals can be our lifesaver.

Family support systems are paramount in this situation. Since the present is the leaner time, whatever you can do to make it more palatable and easier to digest is needed. If the family is able to offer support to this individual in the way of encouragement and validation, the individual will have a greater chance of success. It is hard to be alone in any event.

Consider Bert from Example #2. He is consumed in anger, resentment, perceived inadequacies and bitterness. He does not appreciate help; he believes he deserves it. He will never help others because he maintains a level of anger toward what they represent to him. Any interpersonal relationships he maintains will be self-serving. For example, if he were in a romantic relationship, he would need to be the star. The woman would likely play a "mother" role. She would attend to his every need. He becomes the user, she is the used. He plays the "child", demanding and selfish. Their life together revolves around him. Any offspring only serve to be his rivals for his wife's attention. In a business relationship, he would constantly feel inadequate and try to sabotage his business associate. He would attempt to take credit for the associate's successes while attempting to set the associate up for failure, perhaps even blaming the associate for his own deeds.

What are Bert's needs? The basis of his acting out stems from the low self-esteem he has carried since childhood. This must be addressed before anything else is attempted. Unless Bert truly believes that he is worthy of change, he will allow no change to occur. When self-esteem has been disintegrated and allowed to lie dormant for so long, this can be a significant task. He must evolve to the point that he believes his life is worth something. He must believe he is worth something. Bert's future can be free of the fears that bind him. Once again, look for the Child within Bert who was so tormented. Allow that Child to show anger and frustration. In the present as he discusses the past.

After Bert acknowledges his worth, he needs to address his anger. Anger management is definitely worth exploring. Certified therapists who have received special training in anger management include the letters CART behind their licensure initials. CART is an acronym for Certified Anger Resolution Therapist. Working with a specialist, he will learn to express his anger in more acceptable ways. Many CART's ascertain that anger is never eradicated, simply controlled or contained. However, this takes time to learn and to use proficiently.

The next huge point to address is Bert's relationships. Are they really working for him now that he has self-esteem and can manage his anger? Probably not. At this point, if he is involved in a romantic relationship that is mommy/child based, his partner is no longer receiving what she needs either. She had her own nurturing needs met by becoming the "mommy". Now that Bert is on his way to being an independent man, he no longer desires mommy to smother him. The need for independence has taken over. This may leave his significant other out in the cold. It is likely her needs of being needed and as a nurture/provider are not being met. Honesty must prevail here. If Bert is not able to confront "mommy" about the new rules and boundaries of the relationship, perhaps he should invest in couple's counseling or marriage counseling. With the aid of a licensed professional who specializes in marriage counseling, the situation can be addressed. It is very possible to save this relationship if the couple receives intervention quickly.

If the couple does not seek professional help, and does not communicate regarding these growth changes, the relationship cannot continue meeting the individual needs. When one person in a relationship shows growth, the other must be aware and address this. Mutual growth is always considered positive. When only one grows, the other is left behind. At this point the person is likely to become resentful for what was and what can never be again. For a relationship to be successful, both partners must have their needs met and be generally satisfied. This is a very sensitive topic but very important. When entering counseling, the therapist will explain this to the couple. If overlooked, the relationship is in peril. Dynamic relationships show slow, steady growth for both partners this is considered healthy and optional.
Bert's other relationships probably revolve around work. Since he is so angry and bitter and tries to control everyone, chances of an active

social life are pretty grim. Since Bert is a supervisor, he tends to exploit his power and control over his workers. Remember, by this time, we have addressed his low self-esteem and anger management issues. He is feeling better about himself and controlling his rage. He is in marriage counseling as well. This step should be a natural progression. He is treating himself and his wife with more respect. Only when an individual respects them self, can they truly respect others. Parallels between these should be made. Social skills training is very important here. It will be difficult for Bart to treat others with respect if he doesn't know how.

Old patterns are easy to fall back into. Bert needs to be equipped with a toolbox of social skills. Numerous skills so that if he becomes confused or begins to back-slide, he can reach in and quickly pull out an appropriate skills. One of the worst things to do to someone is to send someone into a potentially explosive situation, where they have failed repeatedly, without safety equipment.

Social skills involve making small talk. What is appropriate? Some brainstorming ahead of time would be helpful here. I wouldn't suggest going so far as to write cue cards, but a little practice beforehand is not bad. Perhaps Bert needs to explore what his coworkers are interested in. Do a little research so the conversation will not be stilted. If they like football, research the state teams and their current statistics. Watch some football. Be ready to name key players and plays.

Discussing new movies at the theater or new releases on DVD will generate conversation. Ask their opinions on gardening supplies or plants that will do well in your area. Everyone has an opinion. Most of us have too many. Unfortunately, many of us seem very eager to share these numerous opinions at the drop of a hat. Take an interest in your coworkers children. Do they play sports? Do the children belong to specific clubs? Perhaps Bert can become involved in a company activity such as bowling or softball, not in an supervisor capacity. He can be "one if the boys" and follow a leader.

Showing respect to others through being interested in their lives, activities, and families is a good place to begin. It is also very important that Bert learn to temper the tone of his voice. Asking a polite question can take on sinister overtones if the tone used is condescending or patronizing. Sarcasm is not a good bet if you are discussing someone's child. Rolling of the eyes, heavy sighs, even apparent distraction can be perceived as rude. Bert needs to practice appropriate body language as well. Lean into the talker to show you are listening. Make eye contact. Do not interrupt the speaker. Ask questions to show an interest. Do not cross your arms at your chest. This is a sign that you want to be elsewhere. Do not work on other materials you may have on your desk when the person enters. Give your full attention to the person speaking. Do not watch the clock not look at your watch. The speaker feels this is a ploy to hurry them, thus showing your lack of interest and concern. Some education regarding leadership styles will be useful. Bert may not know how to lead effectively and appropriately.

The origins surrounding the fear of the past repeating itself are varied. We are not able to identify specific neither home nor academic environments that set this into motion. This fear is based on circumstances and how the individual reacts to them. The personality outcomes are varied as well depending on the traumatic event in childhood that gave birth to this fear. The personalities discussed were developed to cope with the fear, allowing it to stay alive.

We have looked at two scenarios in detail, addressing needs and how to overcome the sabotaging fear. The one thing each person has in common is the fear of the past can be overcome by ensuring a positive future. Each planned their future differently, but each had a *plan*.

When an individual experiences a fear of the past repeating itself, this is partly based on a fear that others would reject, abuse, or eventually attack him. This person will take the offensive stance; he will take the first initiative and move against anyone he believes means him harm. This person often has a history of provoking, attacking, dominating and intimidating parents. If removed to a residential treatment center or otherwise highly structured placement, the movement continues against peers in addition to authority figures. If this behavior is not successfully intimidating, the person may physically move against the individuals. The reason for the eventual physical attack is that of poor alternate coping skills. This person knows no other manner of self-protection.

Due to his primary mode of interpersonal relationships being confrontational, this individual is likely to quickly exhibit anger. There must be a self-defense that combats inadequacy and the feelings of worthlessness. When a person has low self-esteem, it is common for goals set to be unrealistic and somewhat grandiose (usually unattainable and elaborate). When reality threatens to intervene and become the primary focus, the person is compelled to withdraw into a world of fantasy where he is the hero and anything her desires is possible and likely. The need for escape is strong. In a fantasy world, he is in control of everything.

When an individual has such levels of anger and fantasy, the hostility he feels is really toward him, although he will try to make someone else the recipient. When a child or teen can intimidate and dominate the parents, he doesn't have to grow up. He can stay the child indefinitely because he demands the parents will allow this. His inner emotions are responsible for these actions while the individual is responsible for determining the environmental factors that reinforce the actions.

What can we do to stop this unacceptable behavior? If we confront the fantasies, the individual may crash. The person is exhibiting very poor coping skills at this point, which is why he requires the grandiose thinking involving him as the hero, the person in charge.

The individual exhibits an ability to travel to and from the fantasy world as he deems it necessary. This shows us a sense of control. Teaching coping strategies such as positive self-talk, effective communication practices utilizing verbal and narrative skills, goal setting, and establishing a sense of security and safety will be mandatory in order in building his level of control.

When this person interacts threateningly with others, they need to show neither intimidation nor fear toward him. Since this has been his method of taking situational control in the past, if it is to be distinguished, all affect from this behavior must cease. Disruptive behavior does not have to be accepted nor acknowledged. When a person receives a reaction, either positive or negative from the peers/ parents regarding their negative behavior, it often reinforces the behavior. If the person exhibiting the behavior will not remove himself or herself from the proximity, others should remove themselves. It is possible to be in control of others if all others leave. No audience allowed.

Example:

Caretaker: "You are not going to be allowed to eat pie for dinner. You will eat what everyone else does or you eat nothing. If you throw the food on the floor, you will be required to clean it up. [Yelling begins] We are going in another room to eat while you yell. We do not want to hear it.

You **are** better than this. You **can** control this situation better than you are. **When** you would like to be in control, stop yelling. **Then** we can talk."

In this narrative, several steps have been taken. Boundaries have been reiterated: no special treatment, responsibility for behavior and emotional outbursts that do not end with the episode, removal of audience, and a declaration that the behavior is not acceptable. The second half of the narrative is positive and directive. Notice the bold print words: *are, can, when, then.* These are very strong words. The person's self-worth (not behavior) is reinforced, the belief of the care giver in the person's ability is reinforced, and a spoken certainty that the person will establish control is stated. The promise of an impending, future conversation reinforces the love and concern (safety and security) allowed to the individual. The person is reassured that it is his behavior, not his person, that is out of order and unacceptable.

Fear of the Unknown

"I am afraid to begin a new job. What if..."

"I cannot have the recommended surgery. What if..."

"I refuse to try a new hobby. What if I fail? What if I don't like it?"

Fear of the unknown can restrict an individual's life and extinguish future possibilities of success. As humans, we tend to be afraid of things we do not understand or do not know. In small amounts, this aversion can be considered prudent and careful. It is also easy for one to allow these fears to become obsessive, repeating themselves and growing in the process.

Fear of the misunderstood is found in discrimination. Due to a lack of information an individual stereotypes others based on skin color or perhaps a special need. In medieval times demons were blamed for most illnesses. Trephining, drilling a hole in the cranium to allow evil spirits causing discomfort/aberrant behavior to escape, was commonly accepted. People with epilepsy were considered possessed, people with mental disabilities were also considered tools of evil. In Native American cultures, the mentally disabled were considered pure and entities of good luck. Warriors would come together before battle for blessings. History is full of racism, enslavement amongst the major world races. The truth is that society was lacking accurate and meaningful information regarding those they deemed different.

Situation #1

Linda worked in a hardware store for twenty-five years. She knew that she would never be promoted past Floor Sales Assistant, nor would her income increase. She knew the job to be stable and a steady income, albeit a very limited income. Throughout the years competitors tried to lure her away to better positions. As Linda retires at sixty years old, she is tremendously depressed at what she perceives as a life stagnated. She is aware that her fear of the unknown held her hostage. She was afraid to take a chance and afraid to embrace change.

Situation #2

When Estella returned to college at thirty-five, she wanted to drop out immediately. "I walked in the front door and wanted to run out the back," she remembers.

Her fellow students had a median age of twenty-three. She felt old and "out of place". She began to have immense self-doubts about her abilities. Could she learn as fast as when she was younger? Would her memory be sufficient to retain the material? Could she jump back into the college life without embarrassing herself? Through sheer guts and stubbornness, she resolved to do just that.

Situation #3

Surgery is invasive and scary. Even though Amy knew she needed the hysterectomy, she was terrified of all that it implied. Should she have a partial or complete hysterectomy? If only her uterus was removed, would that be more beneficial to her in the long run than if the ovaries were also? Her dream of having children someday were over either way. What would life be like for her without a uterus and ovaries? Would her quality of life be any different? What if she chose not to have this surgery even though the doctor recommended it due to a possible cancerous growth?

If this fear is kept minimal, it encourages the person to research other options, to research possible solutions. Genuine fear warns us to stay alert and pay attention. If the fear of the unknown threatens or jeopardizes us so we cannot do the things we want to or need to, it is detrimental. At this point it is easy to lose focus of the intended goal, focusing instead on the fear and "what if". Each individual has a choice to either embrace the fear, allowing it to engulf and consume the self, or to release it. When we release the fear, we are required to have a certain amount of trust and faith that all will work out for the best. This is called fatalism. When an individual is convinced that there is a higher order, a religious all knowing superior being, the person feels their life is somewhat predestined. Fatalism suggests that one's life is also predestined. What is supposed to happen will. Karma, a balance of good and bad, will be in effect.

To allow one to release the fear that sabotages his/her daily life is one of the strongest moves that can be made. Faith in oneself and the value of one's future is needed. Please understand that even though you are able to release this fear, it may resurface in the future. Each time it resurfaces, you must release it immediately. Fear will emerge from the depths of your consciousness quietly but with incredible force. It is likely you won't feel it rising until it bursts the door down. It is sort of like that big pimple on the morning of Homecoming in high school...we hoped it didn't surface, but here it is larger than ever. The point is you still went to Homecoming and you will still continue to live your life without fear, despite its unanticipated resurfacing.

The fear of the unknown accompanies change, growth, or any new activities. This describes elements in our life that keep it from being boring and mundane. Although it is scary to confront these unknowns, wouldn't it be more terrifying if you didn't? Your life would be the same replay, day after day. There would be no surprises; there would be no plans out of the ordinary, no spontaneity. It is difficult to imagine eating the same supper every night for a month. Imagine the same breakfast, lunch, and supper for a lifetime! You deserve better than that.

"We never know until we try". I remember being told that the author, Stephen King, received over one hundred rejection letters for his manuscript before a quick thinking publisher took a chance. This publisher (and Mr. King) is obviously now happy he did. Many times all that stands between a person and their next move up the ladder of success is a "try". Remaining in the current situation, however comfortable it may be, will eventually become smothering. However, the fear of failure will raise its ugly head here as well. It replays the poisonous adage, "But what if you fail?"

Some people are so afraid that their image will suffer; they are willing to clip their wings and ambitions and play it safely. Perhaps the fear of embarrassment is greater than their need to grow, or so they think. To avoid taking personal risks, individuals often make excuses:

"What would my family think of me if I failed?"

"I need to provide for my children; I must keep the safe position."

"I hate my job but at least it's a known quality."

It is very possible that there is truth in these excuses, to some degree. Yes, it is admirable to support your children. If they are dependent upon you for school, clothes, food, shelter, etc., then it goes without saying that you should adhere to your responsibilities. The point to consider here is that when using this excuse, the conversation should not end there. There is something called problem solving that looks for solutions. Instead of being stymied by any of these excuses, develop a solution that meets your responsibilities while allowing you to confront and overcome your fear of the unknown.

Excuses are a crutch used by people in order to attempt justification and realization of the fear. We seem to feel better about making bad decisions if we tell ourself that it is being done for someone else's benefit, or that our *personal sacrifice* contributes to the well being of others. Notice the words *personal sacrifice.* This is actually the fear that is being masked and redesigned to appear as a positive gesture. When the individual rationalizes that their actions are not self-defeating but martyrish, that they are doing without their dream in order to support and boost a loved one, it is much easier to live with the daily disappointments and unrealized dreams. Overcoming this defense mechanism is mandatory. One should not be allowed to foster these excuses. Reinforcement of these excuses should never be present. Supporting the individual involves eradicating these excuses and rationalizations.

Glasser and Wobbling (1995) have constructed a therapeutic approach that is effective when addressing the pattern of excuses. The basis of reality theory is control theory. This says that humans are motivated to survive and to fulfill four basic human needs: belonging, power, fun, and freedom. The evaluation of the individual's wants, needs, and behaviors, and developing a plan for fulfilling the needs is the process used. When a person perceives he/she is getting what he/she needs from the outside world, these needs are satisfied. If the individual believes something is lacking, the person must generate a *choice* of behavior. This behavior is to close the gap between what a person needs and what the person is receiving. This theory encourages a person to examine the individual wants, behaviors, and perceptions, evaluate them and make an effective plan for the future.

Using reality theory with the fear of the unknown, we see that the individual utilizes excuses as their choice of a behavior solution. It is easier and somewhat safer (it is familiar and well-known to the person) to elect martyrism as opposed to facing and overcoming the fear by confronting the unknown.

Let's address our earlier scenarios:

Situation #1

Linda has retired from her job of twenty-five years. While working at the company, she felt responsible for supporting her family. Every dollar she made was contributed toward family expenses (children, husband, mortgage, etc). At only sixty years of age, Linda realizes she has ample time to pursue another profession. However, now that she has the green light to make a career move, she is terrified. Does she have the skills needed in the "modern" world? She needs technological education. Where does she begin looking for a job? Will her age work against her? It is very luring for Linda to dismiss these fears and just stay at home, telling herself how she has always wanted more time at home for cooking, cleaning, and crafts. The excuses run rampant here. "My husband has always wanted us to have more time together"…"I can save almost as much money as I made by cooking from scratch, sewing clothes, making gifts, selling crafts…" Once again, these excuses are not to be readily accepted at face value. Linda is quickly talking herself out of venturing into the unknown employment sector, preferring to cocoon in the safeness of her home.

Linda is afraid of rejection, feeling miniscule and inept. She is feeling old and useless. This is where the support system must begin. She needs to be redirected when the excuses begin. Once she stops trying to rationalize, she will begin to voice her true fears of inadequacies. These need to be addressed individually with problem solving, offering solutions.

To problem solve the issue of perceived skill inadequacy:

• Do an assessment of what skills Linda currently possesses such as typing, faxing, cash register, credit card machine maneuvering, customer service

• Make a list of what skills Linda would like to learn which she feels would enhance her marketability

• Research where she can learn each skill (community college, secretarial school, a mentor program, senior citizen training programs)

• Assist Linda in developing a professional resume' which capitalizes on current skills and states a willingness to train

• Linda should mail résumé's to businesses she is interested in

Once Linda sees that she is a valuable, productive member of society, the excuses will steadily decline. Once she realizes that she has a lot of offer a business, her self-esteem will increase. There are a number of available senior citizen programs she can become involved in that promote equalization and discourage discrimination. Perhaps she needs information about availability.

Situation #2

Credit should be given to Estella for keeping alive her dream of an education. It appears that she has taken at least one detour on her long-term goal of college, she is now focused and ready to learn. Self-doubts plague her because she has so much riding on this choice. She may have altered her work hours, invested large amounts of savings, and even invested family members as support systems. If she fails, she is afraid of the disappointment of self and others. The only way to never fail is to never try.

Visualizing herself being successful will give her a definitive goal. Many times just the process of visualizing an accomplishment gives the individual the understanding that the goal is accessible. Information is very important to Estella. She does not need the variance of surprise. She must know all details about the college program in which she has enrolled, the expectations of the university, what is required, specifically, for her degree plan, and how much financial aid is available. That is a major perk returning students have that younger do not. There is so much financial aid available to help with childcare and living expenses at there disposal.

Estella sounds like she also has a fear of loneliness wrapped into these uncertainties. She is concerned about not fitting in with her peer group. It is not important for Estella to meld into the twenty-something crowd. She must be willing to present who she really is and abide by her own creed and rules. If she tries to act younger than her years, she will look foolish which will compound her insecurities.

She must approach her peers from her own frame of reference: "I am in my mid-thirties, I have children, and I may be a little overweight. I am here to learn and graduate, not to build a new crew of girlfriends to hang out with." Realizing that academics are her focus, not social acceptance, Estella becomes free from that nagging obligation to be cute and clever, trying to fit in.

Estella needs to make a pro-and-con list. Get a sheet of paper, fold it in half, lengthwise. On the left write "Pro". On the right, write "Con". Under Pro, list all of the positive qualities she exhibits. Under Con, list her challenges (mathematics, procrastination). Make sure she addresses memory abilities, comprehension and listening abilities, even how well she focuses in a boring situation. Can she remain focused on the task at hand if the professor is extremely boring and can she adequately complete a boring reading homework assignment? The list must be completed with the utmost honesty. Remember there is no room for excuses. Either a quality is a Pro or a Con, nothing in the middle.

After completing the list, address each Con, brainstorming a solution to counter the problem. For example, if Estella has a tendency to procrastinate, utilize a daily planner for assignment due dates and begin dates. If a research paper is due October 30, note that in the planner. Note October 1 as the start date for the research paper. It is advisable to make a list of sub-accomplishment goals for the research paper as well: begin research, create a topic sentence, outline paper, collect research for each item discussed in paper, complete rough draft 1, edit and revise, complete rough draft 2, conference with professor regarding paper progress and any last minute questions, construct final draft. Each of these steps should have a due date that must be met.

If Estella lists information retention as a possible problem, she should make arrangements with the professors to utilize a tape recorder during class. This usually requires professor approval. Brushing up on note-taking skills would also be prudent, to maximize her time and information. Once again, utilize the daily planner to list and identify assignment/task dates.

Study skills are also needed. To maximize time and retention, using mnemonics to remember lists, even songs to remember details helps. As horrible as I am in mathematics, I still recall a high school teacher telling me "Soh-cah-toa" (Sign = Opposite, Hypotenuse; Cosign =Adjacent, Hypotenuse; Tangent = Opposite, Adjacent). This is a great use of mnemonics. Use flash cards to remember vocabulary. Put the word on one side, the definition or description on the other. Color-code your flash cards if necessary. There are classes you can take that teach study skills, honing abilities.

By presenting these options to Estella, her fears of uncertainty will begin to minimize. No longer is she uncertain about what to expect doubting her level of performance, she has tools to prepare her for her weak spots. When a safety net is in place, even the most jaded performer is braver. Creating a safety net nullifies the self-sabotaging fear. If one is afraid of failure, and they realize they have a no lose situation, the failure and uncertainty decrease.

Situation #3

Amy is forty years old. She wanted more children. She realizes that her safest option is to have the hysterectomy. Whether it is complete or partial, she will not have the option to give birth. Life without a uterus and ovaries vs. a probable death…why is this decision so difficult? Amy needs to research her two options, evaluate them for merit side-by-side. Adoption possibilities are also reasonable. Amy's fear is not the uncertainty as she thinks it is. Her fear is life with no additional children. Her fear also revolves around her worth as a woman. Putting so much stock in reproduction has led her to misjudge herself. She deserves more credit than she is giving herself.

Is it possible she is dreading the pain of the surgery? The anticipation of physical pain can be overwhelming. Perhaps she has a history of surgeries and is terrified of reliving a past situation. Meeting with the surgeons and her physician prior to the surgery would be advised. Perhaps speaking with someone who has had the procedure done previously would set her mind and fear of pain at ease.

In any event, escaping from the fear by neglecting the operation could be physically compromising for Amy. Her support system should monitor her closely in this manner. Amy may be very capable of postponing the inevitable until it is too late to have any choice in the matter.

Fear of Commitment and Fear of Intimacy

"I realize we have been dating for three years. I just don't feel ready to make this relationship permanent."

"I cannot let anyone through to my personal space."

"My daughter is involved in an abusive relationship. Why won't she leave the guy? I guess somehow I have failed her as a mother."

Although all three of these examples are commonly voiced in reference to a person with fears of commitment and/or intimacy, each is vastly different in scope. The origin is similar. The origin emanates from a lack of security, a lack of self-esteem, and a barrage of earlier childhood issues we will discuss in depth. The scope of each deviates from interpersonal relationships, to individual need, to projecting the fears to one's offspring and her traumatic, unhealthy relationship. Most individuals with a fear of commitment often find it difficult to make decisions in general. All decisions, however small, have something in common…they impact the future. This can lead to many missed opportunities.

This individual is usually in a state of anxiety. They are running from something (their past) or blindly towards something (their fantasy goal) with little regard for the present. These fears are where numerous other fears combine. The fear of commitment can be a fear of committing to anything stable and long term. This includes a profession, a job, or a relationship. The fear of commitment may even involve material objects. The person may be so terrified of the unknown and what may happen in the future that he/she is unable to convince themselves to actually make a long term purchase such as a home or a car. This individual easily exists in a constant state of worry and anxiety about where they are in life and where they are going. Due to the constant state of unrest, the individual is rarely satisfied with self or surroundings. The insecurity associated with this must be decreased as confidence is increased.

Fear of intimacy can negatively impact also to early childhood experiences. Delving into the early familial relationships of the individual would be a prudent therapeutic step. How does the person describe the relationship with his father? His mother? How does he get along with his siblings? Growing up, what types of family activities were indulged? Did the person feel valuable or appreciated by other family members (specifically address the individual relationship with each family member considered a part of the nuclear family)? The nuclear family is comprised of people living in the same home as the individual. One may even blur the boundaries of this to include the family members living not in the designated home with the person, but perhaps across the street if they interact daily.

Fear of intimacy can involve different types of relationships. This fear can stop an individual from developing a deep, personal connection with others. Romantic relationships are considered terrifying by this person, although he/she may initially be most attracted to someone for the very reason they eventually run away from the person. What is unattainable is often attractive. Subconsciously, the individual wants the security and safety of a long-term relationship. Consciously, he/she will sabotage the relationship just to have an easy way provided to get out of it.

Does the individual realize this sabotage? Probably not. The person likely attempts to justify the break up. "I realized she just doesn't have the qualities I need in a mate." Perhaps the individual becomes very critical of the newly departed mate even before the relationship ends. It is probable that the individual began "helpful observations" that hastened the end of the relationship. None of us want to be criticized regularly, even if we are told it is for our "own good". The person who is afraid of intimacy and commitment must fool himself or herself into believing he/she is the hero, the one who was jilted by the bad ex-mate. Once again, it is difficult to maintain an air of innocence and sincere motives when excuses are not allowed. Think of Teflon; this person embodies that surface. All responsibility for negativity and change just slides off.

Situation #1

Jackson is a fifty-year-old bachelor. Desperately craving a family and a reprieve from temporary girlfriends, he is focused on maintaining a long-term relationship. His longest relationship lasted nine months, when he was thirty-seven. He still doesn't understand why she gave him ultimatums and became so bossy. He tried to help her by showing her the faults in her personality and being very honest about his displeasure with her. He seems to do well in his chosen profession as a lawyer.

Situation #2

Lulaylee has been married for fifteen years. She considers herself very lonely, but claims to love her husband. She is unable to share true emotions with him. The couple has no children by choice. She is not trusting of her husband's true intentions and has difficulty believing his level of commitment to her.

Situation #3

Jennifer has an unsuccessful history in relationships. She routinely chooses men who are unavailable emotionally. She blames them for their inabilities then blames herself for her own. She is unable to hold down a job for any length of time. She rarely keeps appointments of any kind. She is looking for someone to take care of her financially and emotionally.

When we are children, our parents are charged with the responsibilities of taking care of us. They are responsible to provide for our physiological needs (food, water), our safety needs (emotional and shelter) and our security needs (also emotional and shelter). Our self-esteem is developed through their treatment of us and our interactions with them as well as society in the early years. What about those of us who experience a traumatic experience as children?

As a child, this person would feel rejected and abandoned by the parents. Growing up, the individual realizes that society is neither able nor willing to provide the tools needed for the healing to begin. Appropriate role models who have overcome similar adversities and made a positive life are hard to locate. The early wounding causes a person to turn the disapproval inward, on the self. No matter what they do, it is never enough, never sufficient. When one tries to resolve the early trauma with continuing a day-to-day existence, it is tempting to take the easy way out. We put on a smile, pretend nothing is wrong, and keep up all appearances.

Psychologically, if we do not address the early feelings of neglect and abandonment, we will keep repeating the pattern of behavior that is counterproductive and self-sabotaging. Unavailable people are the safest choice for this person. Subconsciously they continue to look for this type of individual. Logically, if an individual who fears commitment and intimacy is dating a perpetually unavailable individual, what will the outcome be? Two isolated partners sharing nothing. This is a relationship that is designed to fail. This individual sets himself up to be let down.

Needs

Situation #1

Jackson believes he is entitled to a family. This is his dream and he is confused why it is not his reality. Let's take a look at his relationships. On the job relationships would include the legal support staff and other lawyers. Since Jackson has a fear of intimacy, he keeps coworkers at arm's length. He doesn't want to "get involved" in their daily life drama. He is perfunctory at best in conversation, offering no depth. If someone tells him the child is ill, he'll respond "that's rough" and keep going. He will not ask how he can help nor what medications the child is taking for the illness. These caring questions don't even occur to Jackson. He sees work relationships as distant and feels comfortable keeping them that way. He protects himself from the vulnerability of caring for others.

In his personal life, women are part of a revolving door system. As far back as he can remember, relationships began with a bang, fireworks, even the idealized violin music playing softly in the background. As soon as he became comfortable with the woman, he let down his defenses to a degree. He tries to "help" each become what he sees as an improved version of the original. Obviously, this is counterproductive to a long-term relationship. Jackson is truly baffled by their behavior. However, he is unwilling to look at himself as the cause of the problem. His fear of being judged by others is connected to his belief that he will fall short of the scrutiny. He puts up walls that others are not allowed to penetrate. A wall is built to protect and to keep something threatening from entering something vulnerable.

Jackson needs to explore the true reason for erecting the wall. Is he trying to protect the little boy within who was hurt early in life? Was this child encouraged to love, trust, and depend on an adult who systematically let him down? Now the man protects the vulnerable insides with a fortress wall. Until Jackson can dynamite through the wall, he will remain unable to foster a healthy, equal, interactive relationship. This wall protects him from another traumatic experience. It is a reaction to the uncertainty and unpredictable ness of human nature. Only if he realizes he no longer has a need for the wall will it crumble. Jackson needs to be provided with the safety and security he missed as a child.

Situation #2

Lulaylee is alone, in a partnership, with someone who also feels the loneliness. There is no interaction not emotions expressed. Lulaylee first needs to establish an understanding of her emotional status. Emotions may be pleasant or unpleasant. The pleasant emotions include joy, affection, and fulfillment. Unpleasant emotions include fear, anxiety, and doubt.

Emotions have three basic components. The first is the cognitive component. This includes thoughts, beliefs, and expectations. This component determines the *intensity* of the emotional response. The second is the physiological component. A change in the basic physiology of the individual is due to this. When a person is in a rage, adrenalin pumps, heart rate increases, and blood pressure rises. Often, perspiration drenches the individual and their pupils may dilate. The behavioral component is the third part of the package. This includes a variety of emotional expressions including facial expressions, body postures, and even voice tone.

There are also six general characteristics of emotions. These are:

- When a basic need is not met or is challenged, an emotion is experienced. When a basic need is met or satisfied, an emotion is also experienced.

- Physical and physiological changes occur when an individual experiences an emotion.

- Emotions affect thinking, reasoning, memories, and other psychological activities.

- When a person experiences an emotional state, high energy levels are released. Basically, we experience a fight or flight mode. We immediately determine to stay or run.

- How a person develops and expresses emotions is based on maturation and learning.

- Unpleasant emotions lead to negative response emotions. Pleasant emotions lead to a positive response emotion.

When an individual first experiences an emotion, performance is increased. When the emotion is prolonged, performance decreases.

When Lulaylee experiences fear of intimacy she is saying she does not feel safe enough with her husband to let down her guard. She wants to improve her relationship but also tries to avoid anything that may cause a problem. Since safety and security are a problem, sharing true emotions are also a problem. Lulaylee is trying to improve the marriage by pretending there is *no* problem. Remember, the stronger the emotion, the more intense the motivation.

We know that fear evolves through frustration, trauma, and many kinds of threats. As a person ages, the causation of fear also changes. The basis of her fear may have begun with inconsistencies in security and safety measures with her parents. As she became a teen, these uncertainties evolved into fears involving parental rejection. She wanted to make her parents proud of her. She felt that she owed them. It is common for a child who was neglected or abused on some level, in the very early years, to internalize the blame for such adult actions. The child believes they are guilty in some fashion. As an adult, the person feels that as a child they should not have cried so much, should not have been so needy, or even that they were too expensive for the parents to adequately provide for. In all cases, these are logistical fallacies. A child is not responsible for his/her own neglect. The parent is. For the child, then teen, then adult to harbor these corroding feelings of guilt and blame, is for the child to absolve the adult of wrong-doing.

Guilt is the feeling of self-reproach for believing one has done something wrong. When we make a judgment about our own character or behavior, it stays with us and haunts us. Taking responsibility for one's actions, releasing the self if no wrong was committed, is the secret to overcoming guilt. Allow that people, you included, will make mistakes. If these mistakes were detrimental in someone's quality of life, then an accusation should be directed at the individual. Look at the individual's motives. Did the trauma occur due to a human fallacy? Did the trauma occur due to a human choice? These are different considerations. People often do not know they are making an error until it has been done. In this case, can forgiveness be an option? If the person intentionally hurt someone else, someone helpless, they had a negative motive. People oftentimes try to justify their actions through blaming someone else. This should not be allowed. Confront what happened, analyze motives, and then put it behind you. There is nothing you can do in the present to change the past.

As Lulaylee enters adulthood, her focus remains on playing the worthy daughter, but it begins to generalize. She becomes afraid of failure mall venues, not just the family based situations. If she is not successful, she has let down her parents, again, just as she did as a child (she is carrying the blame). She wants a chance to have a positive relationship, so she marries with the intention that she can work hard enough to make the relationship work. Once again, she is circumventing the crux of the situation…Lulaylee is unwilling, and perhaps unable, to give enough of herself, emotionally, to build a foundation for the relationship. Without a foundation, no secure and safe structure can be erected. She is self-sabotaging. She is setting herself up for repeated failure.

Most behavior and response is cyclical. Lulaylee knows that if she remains sullen and silent for several hours, her husband will inquire as to the cause. This reassures her that he cares about her. She feels she must manipulate the situation in order to receive what she needs from him. She is unable to be honest and straightforward. She cannot say," I need to talk to you and know that you care about me."

These cycles can be very negative, encouraging a passive-aggressive approach. Passive-aggressive is when an individual is indirectly punishing another. The silent treatment, spitting in someone's food when they are not looking, even gossip can fall into this category. This behavior begins a negative cycle that must be stopped. The key is to make it stop immediately.

If Lulaylee's husband responds positively to her passive-aggressive ploy, it encourages her. She is likely to repeat the behavior. If a child is given attention when he throws a temper tantrum in a crowded store, be assured he will do it again. The cycle must be stopped. A correct response to her silence would be, "Honey, if you want something from me, if I can help you in any way, you must use your words and tell me exactly what you want." The individual then excused himself from the area, putting distance between them. At this point, Lulaylee must reproach her husband in a positive and direct manner.

It is prudent to note that while doing these behavioral exercises, the husband must be encouraging and stable. He must be a part of the solution, not the problem. If he does or says anything to encourage a breach in the safety or security of their relationship or of Lulaylee, she will backslide pre-baseline (worse than where she was to begin with). This is not a time for criticism or berating. Positive affirmation is required. Let her know how much her directness is appreciated. Share your own deep feelings and thoughts with her. This opens you up to be vulnerable just as she is at this time. When both partners are exposed emotionally, it is reassuring for each. No longer are they on a sole journey; it is now a journey for two.

Trust is the next issue to explore. Why does she not trust his words? Have his actions, in the past, defied his words? If he has been reliable and honest in the past, where does this trust issue come from? Once again, look back to the childhood.

Trust vs. mistrust is a stage of Eric Erickson's (1963) Psychosocial Stages of Development. In the first year of life, Erickson maintains that if an infant's needs are met on a regular and dependable basis, they develop a sense of basic trust. If not, a crisis will occur which requires resolution. That crisis is the development of mistrust. If a resolution is not readily instituted, this will carry into adulthood. If we carefully explore Lulaylee's early years, we will likely find a series of instances where her mistrust of others has had an adverse affect on her goal attainment and self-image. If one cannot trust anyone else, can they trust themselves? If we can only trust ourselves, whom do we turn to when we need help? What a lonely existence. This is where Lulaylee resides emotionally. She is married and alone.

Communication exercises are recommended. There is a good do-it-yourself manual for couples containing numerous exercises that really work. It's called *Family Interaction Center Series: A Workbook for Building Your Way to a Stronger Relationship* (see additional resources at the end of this book). Lulaylee and her husband must begin to utilize exercises encouraging communication, not just conversation. Conversation is when two people discuss the weather, the news, children, things they have in common, and generally innocuous items. Communication involves feelings, emotions, beliefs, goals, and so many other items that are close to the heart. Marriage counseling is always a good move to assess where the relationship is currently and where the couple visualizes it three, six, twelve months from now. This also encourages the individual to explore carry over emotions from childhood.

Situation #3

Jennifer is looking for someone to take care of her financially and emotionally. Why? Is she not capable of doing these things? Does she just not want to work? It sounds like Jennifer is a very dependent personality who believes that she requires a man to complete her as a whole person.

Children learn behaviors by watching the parents and caregivers. Are her parents married? Did her mother struggle financially or emotionally at some point in Jennifer's childhood? This fear of loneliness and fear of intimacy could have been learned through her own experiences. We know her relationship history has been like Jackson's, a revolving door. When a person is very dependent on another, it can be smothering. Few people want a relationship in which their role is that of babysitter. Adults always look for something specific in a mate, many times the look for a list of specifics. Although some men tend to like the more submissive and docile female, it is helpful for the lady to present these qualities up front, not pretending to be independent just to get his attention. Honesty in relationships is mandatory if they are to last.

Jennifer's anxiety is pronounced. She feels helpless and somewhat hopeless. She is unable to find a solution for her problem because she doesn't understand her problem. It appears that she thinks the problem is her being single. The solution is for her to be taken care of by a man. Her fear that she is experiencing she does not understand. Remember that fears are often based on unresolved issues, which people have routinely shut out of their consciousness. Her anxiety is in the present...what do I do if I am alone, how do I pay my bills if I am alone, what is my worth as a woman if I am alone, what if I never find someone to take care of me...? Anxiety activation can be triggered by the reappearance of the fear. When we are experiencing high levels of anxiety, it is difficult to focus on reality and goal setting. It is easy to get swept under the water, as in an undertow, and become confused as to where the surface is. Anxiety tends to muddle and confuse the situation, as one perceives it.

A dependent individual is terrified of independence and autonomy. Their lack of self-confidence is so extreme that they often have trouble making daily life decisions without assistance. This would explain Jennifer's continual missed appointments. She is determined to find someone to tell her what to think and how to live so she doesn't have to do that for herself. She is not lazy; she has an unrealistic view of security and safety. She wants to be so severely contained that if something goes wrong, it is not her fault. She thinks the severity of the situation will protect her from uncertainties.

There may be a history of maternal neglect in the childhood years of the dependent person. They express a constant need for attention, are passive, show a lack of perseverance, and several oral behaviors (smoking, over eating, thumb sucking, drinking). They tend to be women and the youngest sibling. Prolonged illness can also be a factor in this dependency.
Jennifer has a fear of hurting others by her independence. Why is she afraid of this? Whom is she afraid of hurting? Assertiveness training

is a great idea. She must learn to use "I" statements to ask directly for what she wants:

Jennifer: "If you would buy me an ice cream cone, I'd eat it."

"I" statement: "I am hungry for an ice cream cone. I would like to buy one."

Empowerment of the self, building self-esteem, asking specifically for what the person desires is all a part of assertiveness training. Aggressive and assertive are different, remember. This is discussed in more detail in a different chapter of this book. The bottom line is that it is time to stop allowing yourself, or someone you care about, to be a victim.

Building Jennifer's worth of self is important. It is only by doing this that she can begin to let go of her anxieties. What about her fear of commitment? She is only attracted to unavailable men. These are the safe ones. She doesn't have to worry about a long-term relationship with the unavailable. This is a very dishonest way to venture into the relationship arena. She is pretending to want a relationship when she is terrified of having one.

When we are children, we see ourselves as a part of a larger entity...the family unit. Our parents become our role models. Society becomes our peer group. Robert Burney (1995) ascertains that our parents and society taught us to be dishonest emotionally by wearing different masks for different people. Believing that our parents reflected our individual worth, and that love was conditional on our playing along, we were taught to keep secrets and appear as they wanted us to. He says the parents used fear, guilt, and shame to control the child's behavior to retain their own self-worth. Carl Jung (1939) says that individuals present a persona to others in order to appear pleasing to them. A persona is a mask we wear that hides our true self, yet presents to society an acceptable face. The persona is based on others' criteria of what is appropriate.

In either case, Jennifer, Lulaylee, and Jackson are all presenting themselves as willing to become emotionally vested in a relationship when they are really hesitant about opening the door to vulnerability. Each craves security and stability in a partner but is terrified of the fact that in order to do that, they too must bare all. Our individual self-esteem should not be directly related to society's vision of what we should be or what our lives should look like. Each individual must set his or her own expectations for the present and the future. Set goals of behavior. Everyone is lovable and worth being loved. There is nothing in our past that can deflect that fact.

Material items cannot disguise who we really are and make us more acceptable to others. This value must come from within. The masks or personas that we use so easily cannot fool us. Another theorist, Carl Rogers, (1980), said that when we find our true self, who we really are, it will be a combination of who we think we are and whom we pretend to be. Of course, there is a journey involved to reach the true self. One must carefully explore their situations from childhood to present as we have with Jackson, Lulaylee, and Jennifer. Determine causations for fears. Analyze the anxieties that accompany the fears. Address each need individually, problem solving a solution. Create a short-term goal list and a long-term goal list. Obtain professional intervention to assist you with the trouble areas, those stubborn stains that will not allow them to be removed by you. Sometimes just having an objective observer can help so much in establishing a problem solving approach.

Fear of Abandonment

"If I refuse to allow anyone to get close to me, so when they leave, it won't hurt."

"I'll reject you first; that way, you can't leave first."

"Please don't leave me. I cannot be alone again."

The fear of abandonment is the fear of being rejected by others. It is also when we care deeply for someone and believe whole-heartedly he or she will eventually leave us. Ultimately, they will show disapproval, disappointment and leave. If not, perhaps we will emotionally smother them until they leave. A fear of abandonment is based on the belief that for some reason the individual feels unworthy. The individual believes anyone allowed to enter his/her heart will only break it. With this belief, the person feels he/she must protect the self. In an effort to protect against rejection, it is easy to drive significant others away.

Where do these intense fears originate? We look again to the childhood. It is common that as a child the individual felt unloved or abandoned by a parental figure. Studies suggest that if a father figure is absent, the female child often tries to compensate for the early neglect through exhibitionism or promiscuity as she matures. Feelings of rejection by a parent are also common. When a parent rejects the performance of a child through disappointment or ignoring it, the child either tries very hard to impress the parent or may neglect the performance element all together to punish the parent. The child who chooses to deal with the early years of rejection through exploitation is the person we are addressing in this chapter.

The rejection does not have to be "real". It can be a perceived rejection by the child whom now, as an adult believes to be the truth. Fear of rejection can lead to obsessive ness, clinginess, even jealousy in relationships.

Example #1 is thirty-five years old. She was married once, at twenty years old. She purposely married an older man thinking he would take care of her (dependency). She had planned her future around this man. She quit work, tried to get pregnant, and monitored his hourly activities. When he chose to leave her instead of babysit her, she was once again rejected. Thoughts of inadequacy from childhood became her focus. She perceived his exit as an attack against her, not her behavior.

Growing up, Sue had three older sisters. They were stellar students. The parents gave positive attention to them based on achievements, not on love or affection. Sue struggled in school and struggled with depression. The accolades were not bestowed upon her. Her parents tolerated Sue until she graduated from high school. Her father, a cold and absent man, stressed to her that she needed to get married if she "wasn't going to do anything else with her life." After living with disappointment and rejection, Sue was eager to marry. She clung to her husband for dear life. He was her ticket out of her house and away from her parents and their negativity.

Sue is terrified that he will leave. She is willing to do whatever she can to keep him with her, like a caged animal. She began calling him hourly, while at work, in order to know where he was, what he is doing, and that he is safe. Sue uses baby talk to converse with her husband. He has told her that he married a woman, not a child.

A pattern of emotion and behavior is emerging. Emotionally, she is destitute. She feels alone, helpless, and hopeless. Her true love has left. She has no support system. To whom does she turn for guidance and safety? She feels so alone. These emotions direct her behavior of dependency. She is trying to secure a support system that she can believe in and depend upon. Sue does not understand that the support system she is desperate for comes only from within.

Empowering Sue by teaching her the skills of becoming assertive and independent is a needful task. Assertiveness training is based on taking responsibility for one's own actions. No one can make you feel anyway that you do not choose to. When teaching an individual to be assertive, it is necessary to distinguish between assertive and aggressive. Aggressiveness can get a person hurt or arrested. Aggressive behavior involves yelling (sometimes), threatening others, perhaps even actual assault. Assertive behavior is when one stands up for themselves. This is to be done with a level voice, emotional control, and a carefully considered verbal approach.

Example:

Aggressive: A man is driving his car on the Interstate. A person pulls out in front of him, driving ten miles below the speed limit. Leaning out of his driver's side window, the man yells, "Speed up, you @##$%$#. If you don't get a move on, I'll kick your &**%."

Assertive: The man is driving his car on the Interstate. The same person pulls out in front of him, driving ten miles less than the speed limit. Instead of yelling, the man honks his horn once to alert the driver. He slows down until he can pass the vehicle.

Being assertive can help an individual solve dilemmas. Asking specific questions, addressing one's specific needs, letting others know that you may not be happy with the decision, but you can work with it, are all parts of assertiveness. When you are arguing with your spouse, instead of becoming sullen and passively aggressive, an assertive individual would discuss the emotion.

Example:

Assertive: "You have really hurt my feelings tonight. When you told me, in front of our daughter, that you think my opinions are stupid and worthless, I was humiliated. There is never an appropriate time to embarrass me. If you truly believe these things, we should discuss this privately."

The assertive approach is preferred and generally promotes a more positive outcome that sitting silently and sulking due to what the spouse said. If the problem is not addressed specifically, how will it become resolved? It is important to always remember, though, that before you ask a question, make sure you really want to know the answer. If you ask your spouse how much she loves you as you are arguing, her truthful answer may be "none". Try not to set yourself or your partner up for failure. Most of us feel we love our significant others more at certain times, like when we are getting along or sharing a special moment, than when we are angry at them.

Being assertive is not having permission to bully others. It is giving you permission to be honest and direct while trying to do no harm to others or self.

Example #2

Sherri is an exotic dancer. She is very talented and makes good money. She is twenty-eight years old and she has no intention of maintaining a monogamous relationship. She finds great pleasure in dating many men, enjoying gifts and attention from them, then discarding them. She goes home to an empty apartment and cries, not knowing why the emptiness inside doesn't go away.

This fear of abandonment sounds very similar to the fear of commitment. The fear of commitment has several bases, this being one of them. Sherri didn't have a close relationship with her father. He left the house when she was three years old. Her mother worked long hours to provide for her. Sherri learned at a young age that her beauty attracted men. Older men had money to buy the items she wanted as a child. She dropped out of high school before graduating in order to begin her dance career. When these men, her customers, give her money and material goods, she gets a smug satisfaction. It is easy for her to feel they "owe" these things to her, just as her father does. It is easy for her to displace her abandonment fears of her father with the exploitation of these customers.

When Sherri cries due to the loneliness within, this is due to the fact that she is not confronting the fear or the cause of the fear. She is trying to ignore it, even go around it. Sherri needs to address her absent father and the pain this has caused. Does she really know why he left? What specifically could he have provided that her mother did not? Why does she blame her father? What specifically did he do to hurt her? What is the purpose of her revenge? Does Sherri realize that she is minimalizing herself when she minimalizes the importance of her customers? She is the bait, they are the fish. She reels them in just to cast them back out. Why doesn't she realize that she deserves to feel better about herself than that?

Since Sherri was three when Dad left, she doesn't know the real reason. It is possible that Mom never shared the truth because she was so young, when her parents separated. Maybe Mom was so hurt and angry with the man leaving that she was unable to attend to the child's need for answers of some sort. Sherri needs to go to her mother and try to resolve this issue. She must have closure to his leaving *as a child.* Sherri must know that she did nothing to precipitate the Dad's absence. This addresses the guilt issue again. Sherri appears to carry quite a bit of guilt over the leaving, not so much the parents splitting up. The Child within must be forgiven for what she believes she did wrong so she can move on.

Other than providing a father figure, what does Sherri think Dad could have provided in the earlier years? Perhaps more financial stability. Maybe Dad's presence would have provided time for a relationship between the two of them to develop...playing games, enjoying sports together, maybe just "hanging out". Dad's presence may have made it so that Mom wouldn't have needed to work so hard. It is also possible that Sherri has romanticized the dream of Dad. In her child-driven fantasy, Dad would be her hero. He would inadvertently free her and Mom from the struggles and hardships they had to endure. This fantasy vs. reality needs to be explored. The fantasy Dad is probably nothing close to the real Dad. She will be disappointed when she realizes dad is only mortal and has flaws and weaknesses. Children need a hero. She wanted him to rescue them. Perhaps she still wants someone, Dad-like, to rescue her.

This hero is simultaneously the villain. He ran out on them! He is to blame for the nights of no dinner, the lack of new clothes and new shoes. He was the villain because he took everything that could have made her childhood pleasant. If only...Sherri needs to dispense with the "if only" mode of thought. Her love/hate emotions toward Dad give her excuses to act however she chooses. It is easy to blame Dad for not being around. Using men is a type of vengeance toward Dad. What is her opinion of men? It is very possible that she sees them as inferior and users of women. This is how she rationalizes that it is acceptable to use them first. This should be addressed as well.

When Sherri targets her customers for her own gain, she transforms herself into the bait. Is this dehumanizing? It depends on Sherri's perspective. If Sherri is able to maintain her dignity and self-esteem, if Sherri is not out to "use and abuse" others, then why would it be dehumanizing? If Sherri is on a revenge mission, seeing these men as animals being led to the slaughter, then what worth does the bait have?

Lawrence Kohlberg (1981) developed a classic theory on morality. He has established stages of morality based on why one makes the decisions they make. He ascertains that it is not so much *what* a person does, but *why* the person does it. This is the same approach we are taking with Sherri. If Sherri's reasons for her actions are due to anger, low self-esteem, and striking back, then nothing positive will come of it. This is a certain way to destroy the self. It is very important that her reasons are explored and addressed.

Just because her father never told her she didn't deserve better, doesn't mean it's true.

Example #3

Jonathan sees his girlfriend talking to another man. The man is a friend of hers from work. Jonathan storms over to the pair, pulls her roughly by the arm until they are far away from the friend. At night, he has recurrent nightmares centering on infidelity. He is convinced that she will leave him.

Jonathan's lack and need of security is very similar to Sherri's. He is expressing it differently. Instead of being overtly dependent or using women in general, he is exhibiting a different type of independence born of insecurity. Jonathan is extremely jealous and believes that if he can express it overtly, he can bully or scare his girlfriend into staying in the relationship. He is obsessed with the thought of her leaving him, never understanding that he is continually pushing her away with his aggressiveness and doubts.

This behavior is not based on reasoning. It is based on feeling. These emotions come from the belief that he is insufficient and unworthy to love. It is likely that he spends a lot of time looking for reasons that she should reject him and evidence that he is being rejected.

This would cause him to begin to blame her for bizarre things. He would be adamant that he saw her flirting with someone at the grocery store, that he heard her dial someone on her cell phone but quickly hang up when he came in the room. Incorrectly blaming her, issuing accusations, perhaps even threatening her would be probable behavior for Jonathan to exhibit.

This is a pattern of behavior that Jonathan must break. His fear of abandonment is involving anger. When one physically threatens another, by pulling the arm so hard the body moves, the intensity of the interaction is greatly increased. This is no longer a fear to be dealt with. It is a possible behavioral escalation that can lead to violence.

When we look at the statistics of women who have been abused and their abusers, we see the "causation", from the male perpetrators, to lean toward feelings of insecurity. We all know that just because someone feels they may be abandoned there is neither reason nor justification to hurt another. Many abusers, after admitting the aggression and anger problems, also mention the feelings of hopelessness and helplessness they are experiencing in the relationships. Due to fear of rejection and abandonment, they believed the woman must be made to stay, by any means necessary.

The feeling of abandonment is addictive. The emotional drama involved with repeated heartache can be consuming. This individual may constantly pursue the hard-to-get partner in order to keep the relationship exciting. Unless the individual is pursing someone they are insecure about, love is not felt. When one is attracted to this individual, it is common for the person to be pushed aside because the relationship maintenance is of prime importance. The love-interest is unable to deal with a "real" relationship that involves emotions and commitment. The "fantasy" partner, the unattainable one, is much safer.

Being attracted to someone also initiates the reality that you may lose the person. This can be terrifying and cause one to pull back. A fear of engulfment may also exist in the fear of abandonment. This occurs when someone is pursuing the individual with abandonment issues. The pursued feels engulfed by the other's desire to be together. Panic and emotional shut down occurs. The fear is due to the realization that you may not be able to fulfill their expectations or needs. The concern becomes very egomaniacal, "How can I keep my own identity when she needs part of me to validate her?" Abandonment of one's own needs is overwhelming to this person. The individual would rather run and hide than maintain the relationship.

When one is so afraid of rejection that relationships are abandoned completely, one becomes socially isolated. Sometimes a negative attraction is more compelling than a positive one. In this case, the individual becomes involved in dysfunctional relationships that are unhealthy. There is usually a taker and a giver in these relationships. Rarely do both partners share. The relationship remains skewed until it disseminates. This individual prefers the negativity. This way the fear of engulfment, the fear of permanency, the fear of a relationship, is taken care of.

Insecurity increases with each romantic rejection. When one experiences a series o rejection, the self-esteem is affected. One begins looking to others to replace the self-esteem within. Powerlessness is experienced. Each time the person reaches to an unavailable partner, the self-esteem is destroyed. The cycle replays. Due to such an absence of self-regard, one becomes unable to respond to the positives. A compliment, an affirmation, will be lost on this individual. They feel so undeserving, the reinforcement I disregarded.

If this individual happens to become successful in the relationship arena, and becomes comfortable, he/she is likely to shut down. The chase and unavailability is what drives the person. The fear of having an honest relationship that involves trust and respect is very real.

Needs

To address the needs of someone experiencing the fear of abandonment, we must address: self-esteem, self-regard, and dynamics of a healthy relationship, security, and communication. So many other factors are involved in this fear. Family history is very important. We must be able to retrace the years, to discover when the individual first felt neglect and alone. It is also important to look at the fear of rejection. When a person is confident of eventual rejection, this is often found to be learned somewhere at some point within their life. We must explore the individual's history to find when this was initially learned. Look at the follow ups to the rejection as well; what are the individual situations that confirmed this fear? It would be a good idea to consult the chapter on *fear of the past repeating itself*. There are many good tips for dealing with this component of abandonment.

When a person has low self-esteem, they feel undeserving of anything good. The person believes that they deserve items/ treatment of lower quality.

"What have I done to deserve such nice things?"

"Take this back. It's too nice for me. I don't deserve it."

The individual does not acknowledge positive comments. If given a compliment about their person, they believe it to be insincere. The individual does not feel any ownership of positive attributes. Very common responses to such a compliment include a smirk, rolling of the eyes, even a cynical reply, "What do you really want?" It is imperative to assist the person in building their self-esteem and improving the self-perception. Positive comments should continue. Make sure the compliments are sincere. Insincerity could do a tremendous amount of damage to this individual. If insincerity is identified, it justifies the initial suspicions of lack of trustworthiness. The individual with abandonment fears will need validation on feelings and fears. Insincerity is caustic to helping the person overcome this.

It is also important to note that reliability is needed. If you are making plans to do something with this person, follow through. If you are not reliable, if you do not show up on time or allow something to "come up" that changes the initial plans, this individual is likely to not allow you another chance at redemption. The person truly believes you will NOT show up for the date, you will NOT be trustworthy in the relationship; you WILL let her/him down if they have faith in you, and you WILL eventually leave them. Remember that the person is looking for an excuse to validate these emotions. If you are trying to help the person, do not allow negative validating situations.

Attachment

Since we have discussed the absentee father and the effect it can have on a female in later years, I would like to discuss the concept of attachment as it impacts all of us psychologically and emotionally. A child raised in an institution without stimulation and attention of a regular caregiver or locked away at home being abused or neglected us often withdrawn, frightened, and speechless. Even if the child is eventually raised in a positive environment scars of these deprivational years remain.

Most abusive parents report being neglected or abused as children. Lewis (1988) reports a study involving fourteen young men awaiting execution for juvenile crimes. All but two of them had histories of brutal physical abuse. Thirty percent of children who are abused in turn abuse their children.

Severed attachment bonds produce a sequence of behaviors beginning with agitation, followed by a deep sadness, emotional detachment, and then eventually a return to normal living. When a child is exposed to the removal of one parent through divorce or separation, the response of the child depends on the individual's temperament, the intensity of the earlier parental conflict, and the continuity of other stabilizing relationships the child may have. The child may grow up with a reduced feeling of well-being. They are more likely to divorce as adults and have a more difficult time staying upbeat. The U.S. Census Bureau for the National Center for Health Statistics report that children of divided parents are about twice as likely to experience a variety of social, psychological, or academic problems. Most of the children do fine in spite of this, however, if their support system is solid. Friends, mentors, clergymen, relatives, etc. combine a strong system to rely upon.

A child who is experiencing abandonment often acts out due to unresolved issues with rage and grief. If these same issues continue to not be resolved during childhood, the adult is likely to do the same. Validating the feelings, helping the individual express the feelings in appropriate ways, and protecting others from the anger are ways of helping the person confront this issue. Affirming the past helps create a continuity with the past and a direction for the future. The adult should be encouraged to express and acknowledge the situations early in life that have led to the fears of abandonment and low self-esteem. Encouragement is needed to help the person continue this arduous journey.

Since rage often stems from unresolved abandonment issues, there exists within the individual a wealth of experiences that must be processed. This is time consuming and can be repetitive. As the individual tries to make sense of the childhood trauma, he/she will repeat the situation, looking for clarity. Be patient with him/her. This processing is important to the individual understanding the past and being able to put it in the present perspective.

The loved ones who have a family member experiencing abandonment issues are often victims. It is very frustrating to see someone so tormented with fears of the past and future that they cannot live effectively in the present. It seems no matter how hard you try, whatever you do is not enough. Reassurance, support, encouragement, even redirection is exhausting to maintain on a daily basis. Please remember that it took years for this fear to develop to the intensity it is now; it will take a long time to break it back down. Therapeutic intervention is helpful for all involved. The licensed therapist can offer support to the support system as well as direction to the client.

Helping your loved one develop self-reliance and security of self are your goals. Empowerment is needed to readjust the self-concept. Self-esteem building sets the foundation for these other goals to be built. It is helpful to set short-term goals as well as long-term goals for behavior. Short-term goals would involve the person taking a trip to the market and not being in control-you drive there, you pay for the food, and you control aspects of the trip. If the individual is a dependent personality, another short-term goal may be to have him/ her pay the household bills with no assistance. Long-term goals are goals that you want to observe happening three to four months from now. For the dependent personality perhaps the person is no longer apologizing for having an opinion, but instead is stating the opinions regularly without hesitation. For the independent personality, he/she daily takes an active and sincere listening role in how the partner's day evolved, his immediate well-being. Even with the ultimate goals of self-reliance and security, many smaller goals are met along the way.

The fear of abandonment is a huge deterrent in the development of trust. The individual is so consumed with the thought that the significant other will eventually desert them that when the loved one makes an innocent slip-up, it is easily and often misinterpreted as something sinister and insidious. Even as their trust begins to slowly develop, the fear that they will soon be unmasked as unlovable and unworthy remains an almost obsessive preoccupation.
As the relationship builds, the person is encouraged to look at the therapist (or caseworker) as a source of help during the crisis. The people are actually taught alternative methods of behavior that are counteractive to the old ones involving dependency. These people

create a crisis-based lifestyle for their family. What is a minor incident to others becomes a major crisis to them. These people need someone available to offer reassurance and direction if they are to develop completely enough to handle their life challenges. Ask *how* the individual is feeling and what is going on in *their* life. The source of distress is often confusing to isolate and a quick resolution is not to be anticipated. What is causing this person to feel unloved, criticized, or abandoned?

In time, the individual should learn to analyze his or her own situation: what started the anger and what initiated the frustration. Praise should be offered for the ability shown to reach out and get help. Encouragement and approval (positive verbal reinforcement) for doing something to help herself and her situation should also be offered. Just by reaching out, the person is showing dramatic improvement. When an adult is experiencing a fear of abandonment, it is often the result of many years of neglect of the self-needs. Their worthlessness and failures have been repeatedly reinforced. In order to reverse this, the entire pattern of behavior and thought processes must be reversed. This is called repetitive patterning.

Support this person and his/her endeavors. Listen to their memories and fears for the future. Encourage the adults to take time for themselves, away from the children. This is very important in the refocusing and tolerance aspects. If the adult is fearful that the future will repeat the past, the immediate presence is overlooked. She often misses the present. If children are involved, they are all about what is happening in the present. It helps to remove the self from the hotbed of crisis (home or work) for a few hours to rest and return with an unbiased and fresh outlook then confront the issue at hand.

When trying to establish a relationship of trust, one must be able to be honest. Honest emotions include anger and disappointment. When this individual tries to express these directly, to someone significant in his/her life, it is almost impossible. Fear to express anger for fear of reciprocated punishment or abandonment is primarily on the mind of this person. "I cannot tell him I am angry that he stayed out all night. He'll leave me if he gets angry."

The person must be taught that others who care about them will learn to accept their anger, legitimize it, and work out a solution. In this case, it is helpful if a third person, non-related but yet invested (a therapist or caseworker), is involved. Methods of communication are taught and utilized. Reaffirmation of commitment is always present. This way the individual is taken, using gradual steps, to a new level of understanding. From this develops trust.

Remember the importance of acknowledging the individual's accomplishments. So little has been positively reinforced in their lives; they must be told what they are doing correctly as well as what needs to be worked on. Show approval and give encouragement as often as you can. Sensitivity runs high with this group. Many positive intentions by you may be misconstrued as criticism and allegation-based. Consider your word choice carefully to avoid negative comprehension.

Attachment and Personality

Attachment is defined as the emotional bond that forms between an infant and the caregiver. The infant begins to develop an emotional security with this person which can affect the development of future relationships. According to Bowlby (1961), as time passes, an affectionate bond develops supported by a history of "consistent, sensitive, responsive care by the parent". Children form a lasting bond with the caregiver which forms a long-lasting foundation for future interpersonal and romantic relationships. A set of expectations of behavior is developed at his early stage and will last indefinitely.

This caregiver does not have to be a parent. It can be any individual who spends time with them. Toddlers, usually in North America, who spend days at daycare and sleep alone often develop a connection with a cuddly toy or blanket instead of an adult. In the past, it was believed that the person feeding the infant would be the bonding focus. Recent studies show that babies learn through experience to prefer the accompanying stimuli to feeding such as cuddling, warm body contact, eye contact, verbal communication. Even if the infant ceases to see the caregiver once an attachment has been established, the desire to see them remains. Once an attachment forms, it persists.

Separation anxiety is common amongst infants who have developed an attachment bond. Toddlers use parents as a base from which to venture on explorations. If that base is absent, the toddler should experience a level of anxiety. Attachment is stable over the first two years of life through age six. Stability is affected when the family experiences a major life change of events. If the parental employment status changes, parents divorce, death of a loved one close to the nuclear family occurs, etc., the child's stability will be altered simply due to the family dynamics changing. When a parent is distraught and has high anxiety, the child will receive those emotions. Research suggests that children who possess a disposition to stress in early infancy are likelier to develop an insecure attachment later in life.

Not all attachment bonds are identical. An infant is able to develop a different attachment bond with each adult and caregiver in his life. The level of sensitive care giving is very distinctive as to the level and intensity of bond formed with the caregiver. If one caregiver is more removed emotionally and not as overtly sensitive to the child's needs, the attachment will not be as intense as the one formed with the other caregiver who is highly sensitive and attending. Caregivers must modify their behavior to fit the infant's needs. If the mother's ability to do this is confined due to her own restrictions and neediness, the child is at risk of developing a difficult temperament or attachment insecurity. It is the responsibility of the adult to adjust actions based on the baby's responses and needs.

Concepts of creating a secure base, a foundation, and appropriate dynamics of the caregiver/infant relationship will play an important role in how the future relationships develop in the infants' life. Many lonely adults report troubled childhood relationships with parents and either distant or overly enmeshed relationships with romantic partners. This suggests that attachment history influences adult loneliness. The formation of a bond is described as falling in love loving someone or grieving over someone. When this bond is not challenged, it becomes a source of security. Affectional bonds are based on one's emotions.

When a child perceives a symbol of attachment to be close by and accessible, he feels safe, secure and confident. He is able to explore and interact in his environment in a secure manner. When a threat is perceived by the child, feelings of anxiousness or fright occur and he seeks the attention of the caregiver. When the child feels comfort, safety and security, attachment seeking behaviors cease. Based on one's history, the adult's attachment styles are formed. These are influenced by one's belief of self and close relationships. As an adult, one needs a "secure base" according to Hazan and Shaver (1987).

Bowlby and Ainsworth (1978) have determined attachment styles, which heavily influence our partner selections. Adults who want a long-term relationship identify care-giving qualities they want in a mate. Although people tend to want a mate with positive qualities such as kindness, attentiveness and honesty, it is suggested that whom we ultimately end up with are partners who confirm our true beliefs regarding attachment and relationships. Beliefs and expectations we hold before engaging in a relationship affect how secure we are in the relationship. When one is anxious, mistrust, hostility and rejection are projected; when one is secure, positive intentions are projected.

As people are together longer, the levels of anxiousness tend to decrease. Safety should take its place. As time passes, partners become more similar in security levels. Secure individuals have higher self-esteem and tend to be considered as sell-adjusted and caring by peers. Depressed visuals tend to report themselves as insecure.

Attachment Styles

The basic assumption in attachment research of infants is that when the parent responds sensitively to the infant's needs, the infant responds by developing a secure attachment. The lack of sensitive responding by the parent or caregiver results in insecure attachment. *Secure infants* want proximity or contact with the caregiver and will greet the adult at a distance with a smile, yelp or wave. The child with an *avoidant attachment* will avoid the caregiver. The infant who is *resistant/ambivalent* will show hostility toward the parent/caregiver wither passively or aggressively.

Ainsworth established a three category scheme to organize individual differences based on the way adults think, feel, and act in romantic relationships. Hazan and Shaver elaborated on his theory. They determined that when people self-reported n romantic attachment patterns; it was related to belief about love and relationships as well as early memories of parental experiences.

Based on previous studies, approximately one half of the individuals describe themselves as *securely attached*. These characteristics include:

- More trusting

- Less lonely

- Have a history of long-term relationships

- Easy to get close to others

- Dependable

- Positive, optimistic

- Seeks social support when needed

- Positive self-esteem and regard for others

- Sees self as worthy and lovable

The second attachment style is called *avoidant.* These characteristics include:

- Less invested in relationships

- Wary of depending on others

- Engages in more casual sex

- Tends to have experienced childhood trauma

- Is not comfortable with self-disclosure by self or others

- Exhibits lack of intimacy

- May be hostile or verbally abusive when feeling provoked

- Recalls previous relationships as negative

- Tends to work excessively to avoid relationships

• Exhibits difficulty in trusting others

• Becomes nervous when others become too close

• Is not comfortable being intimate

According to Bartholomew (1990), the avoidant individual can be further analyzed as fearful avoidant or dismissing avoidant. The fearfully avoidant person try to avoid being hurt or rejected by the partner. Dismissing avoidants try to maintain a defensive sense of self-reliance and independence as a mode of self-preservation.

Anxious-ambivalent is the third attachment style. Approximately twenty percent of individuals fall into this category. These people tend to have an underlying abandonment fear which makes them crave their significant others to become involved in a consuming relationship. These individuals often remark that their partner is not as invested in the relationship as they desire. The characteristics are:

• Often feels under-appreciated

• Unstable self-esteem

• Insecure in devotion of others

• Has dreams of success but cannot sustain efforts

• Prone to mood swings

• Afraid of separation and death

• Exhibits hostility and anger

• Perceives parents as unfair and intrusive

- Perceives significant other as unsupportive

- Jealous and untrusting of others' intentions

- View partners In negative light after conflict

- Perceives relationships as having less love, commitment and mutual respect

- Frequent involvement in love-hate relationships

- Often doubts the love and dedication of partner

- Often scares others away due to immense need of consuming relationship

In adult relationships, at any one point either partner can be described as stressed or threatened in some regard. At that time, the other partner tends to accept the caregiver role characterized by being more helpful, attentive, or protective. These roles are frequently interchanged as the partner's needs change. The two behaviors of sexuality and attachment influence the other. When an individual is tired, stressed or experiencing anxiety he/she often forgoes sexual activity. This can affect the relationship is the other partner is not empathic to the situation. Attachment can be affected by the interplay of sex and level of care giving. If one partner is angry with the other regarding sexual activity, the attachment between the two will be affected as well. Ultimately, we see attachment, care giving, and sexual behaviors as equal parts of the romantic relationship.

Children's Fears

"I am afraid of the dark."

"Monsters live under my bed."

"I am afraid that if I am bad, mommy or daddy will leave."

Children will experience different fears at different ages. The normal fear experiences are as follows:

Infant and toddler

If a parent is out of the child's visual range, the child thinks the parent has left.

When the bathwater drains from the bathtub, the child believes he/she will go down the drain as well.

When a parent alters their appearance with a hat, a costume, a scarf, etc., the baby may not recognize the parent.

A loud noise may consume them (the dryer, blender, vacuum cleaner, etc).

Older children

When a barber cuts their hair, the child may believe that a part of him will also be discarded with the hair

While at the doctor, a shot may create permanent damage (deflate the child, leave a large protruding hole from which he'll bled to death).

Afraid of worms in their tummy due to eating raw potatoes; afraid of orange trees growing in their tummy because they swallowed an orange seed.

Monsters will emerge from the closet or under the bed when the lights are cut off.

The shadows out side the window will "get them" when it is dark.

Why do children experience these fears? Each fear is based on reality. The baby has not reached the stage of cognition where he is able to discriminate between out of sight and out of place. The child has not mastered the concept of measurement or conservation. He does not understand that his entire body will not fit down the drain or down the toilet. If he is having a bowel movement and flushes the toilet, it seems logical to him that if the feces goes down the pipes, so should he.

The very young child, attached to the parent figure in most cases, feels a sense of safety around this figure. If the appearance of the figure is altered in any manner, the child is not able to process the change.

Consider our infant looking at his mother in a Halloween costume: The child thinks, "The voice sounds like mom's, the hair looks like mom's, but what is that mask covering the face? Mom must have left me alone with this strange woman. I am now terrified. Where is my mommy?"

If a machine makes a loud noise, it will startle or scare the child. The child will perceive the loud noises as loud and scary. When the child is scared, they retreat and try to avoid the danger source (adults do this as well when they perceive danger sources). The child will likely avoid the source until the fear subsides and they are able to cognitively process the connection between item and item use.

When a toddler becomes concerned about getting a hair cut, physician shots, or any activities that involve the preservation of the body, this means the child is becoming aware of body parts. Coupled with the development of an imagination, this knowledge can become quite intense. The imagination is also the basis of the monster theories. Around three years of age, the child leaves the earlier fear of "what is" and becomes afraid of "what could happen if..."

It should go without saying that the child's environment will have much to do with fear development. Under no circumstances should a young child be allowed to view scary movies with violence. The parent should never threaten the child that the monsters will get him if he's not good nor with any supernatural aspects of discipline. This obviously feeds into the fears the child is entertaining, helping them to gain definition, design, and details. The fears can become gigantic and overwhelming when a steady diet is provided.

A parent cannot keep the child from fear development. This is a normal part of cognitive and social development for all of us. The parent can assist the child in facing the fear and putting it in perspective. Do not quickly dismiss the fear as stupid. If it is significant enough to scare your child, it is significant enough for you to take time to address it logically with the child. Before a doctor's visit (or dental visit), take the child to the physician's office and let them look at the items there. Children, like adults, are afraid of what they do not understand. Foreign objects and people can be quite terrifying if you have never encountered them nor discussed their existence. Allow the child to meet the physician and staff. The child should be allowed to look at the waiting and examination rooms. Familiarity encourages safety and confidence.

Using this same approach when you visit somewhere overnight is suggested. Allow the child to explore the room where he will be sleeping. Look in the closets and under the bed with the child. Allow the child to spend time in the room during the daylight hours, with you and other "safe" adults, to establish the familiarity he needs. Encourage your child to sleep with his safety item (doll, blanket, stuffed animal) in this new room. It is always advisable for the parent to be close by the first night in a new place. If the child cries or yells, the parent should make haste getting to the child. This shows the child is not really alone, even though he may be alone in the room. This is a reinforcer of security for him.

Never force a child to enter a situation he may fear. If the child exhibits a fear of heights, do not force him to ride a ferris wheel. If the child is forced to get on the ferris wheel in spite of his protests and obvious terror, this borders on an abusive approach. Therapeutically, there is a technique called implosion where the client is saturated with the feared item. This is done under careful and experienced observations. When a parent forces a child to stay locked in a closet for the purpose of "confronting" his fear of small spaces, the child will react to an extreme. The child is not equipped to deal with this huge input of sensation of the feared object. The parent is not trained to handle the result.

When a child becomes afraid, remove him from the situation. Once you are away from the object of fear, explain to the child why the fear is not real. Use logic and child-friendly words. Do not lecture the child nor use a condescending tone. We want to encourage the child to talk about the item and why it evokes fear within. Once the child can express the fear verbally (drawing also works), you can explain why the item is not to be feared.

Example:

Child: I am afraid of being alone in grandma's bathroom.

Parent: I will stay in the bathroom with you while you use the toilet (turns back to child to allow privacy).

Parent: Now that you are finished, why don't we go for a walk outside and have a talk?
(Remove the child from the feared bathroom in order to discuss the fear.)

Parent (once outside and walking): What is it about the bathroom that scares you? You aren't scared in the bathroom at home.

Child: The floors are old and wood. I might fall through them.

Parent: Would it help if I put a towel on the floor, in front of the toilet, when you need to use the bathroom at grandmother's house?

Child: Yes. If I don't see the old wood, I shouldn't fall through it.

It is advisable that once the fear has been diminished, that the parents and child have a discussion about the fear. The child needs to know that just because wood appears old and worn doesn't mean that it is rotten enough to fall through. By the same token, the parents must acknowledge the fact that wood does rot and can be dangerous. This difference needs to be addressed as well so the child doesn't think that he is out of line and being ridiculous by his speculation and fear. It would be a good idea to allow the child to eventually see others walking safely on the wood floor, perhaps the child walking on the floor holding a parent's hand for safety and security. If the child is old enough, a trip to a flooring center to view different types of wood flooring and the process of installation would be helpful. Information and knowledge can easily decrease fears. Remember, we are afraid of what we do not understand. The more knowledge one gains about the item, the less fearful it becomes.

When a child has been around a variety of people from the infancy stage, he/she is less likely to develop fears. The development of independence and outgoingness seem to lessen the development of fear. Most children crave structure. Around age two, the child is very sensitive to change in locations and caregivers. Gradual steps must be taken in order for the child to develop a sense of security. Allow the new person to just be around the child for a few days without trying to care for the infant. The child will develop trust; at this time, the caregiver can begin gradually caring for the needs. Start by leaving the child for half a day, and then gradually work up to a full day of separation.

If the child becomes anguished about going to bed due to impending separation, sit with the child until he falls asleep for reassurance. A panicky child can stay awake for hours, getting worked up emotionally and wearing out the parent. The child must be comforted by addressing the anxiety.

When a toddler is frightened by separation (or anything else) he believes his parents are as well. When a parent responds with guilt or overreaction to the child, this heightens the anxiety felt by the toddler. For the parent to run into the infant's bedroom at each murmur is not recommended. When a child needs the security of a parental presence to alleviate anxiety, this is different than the hovering parent who quickly responds to each expression of displeasure. The parent is advised to always provide the needed security and safety that a child request. While doing this the parent needs to be upbeat, confident and guilt-free. Encouraging the child, complimenting the effort shown, is recommended as the child tries to become safe and secure with out parental support. Eventually autonomy and independence is our goal.

It is not recommended that parents allow children to become fixtures in their bed at night. The child needs to be trained to stay in its own bed. If the parental protectiveness is encouraging the child's dependency, this needs to be quickly addressed. By age two, the child is no longer an infant and should be experiencing some levels of independence.

I had the opportunity to work with a family who was involved in this cycle. The daughter was five and was sleeping with mom most nights. The daughter said she had nightmares at first, but they "quit when I started sleeping with mom". Mom was not uncomfortable with this arrangement.

After much discussion, mom admitted that she liked the daughter to sleep with her. The parents were separated and mom didn't like sleeping alone. She was encouraging this dependency. She also encouraged all three of her children to converge in her bed on Saturday evenings to watch movies. Her bed was the family meeting place. The five year old daughter rarely slept in her own bed anymore.

Other dependency issues began to surface. The daughter began experiencing separation anxiety when away from mom. Developmentally, this should have disappeared years earlier. Once the bed sharing began and became "normal", other behaviors resurfaced. We had to get the daughter back in her own bed and re-establish boundaries which encouraged independence. Mom and daughter both benefited and grew emotionally from the intervention.

The pre-school child has a specific set of worries. Worries about disasters are common. "What would it be like to…get lost, be separated from mommy for a very long time, to fall out of this carseat, to have the house catch fire...". This age group often worries about very improbable things happening. These fears encompass the parents, siblings, even family pets ("What if the dog bites me...What if the dog eats me..."). This child worries about injury. This is the age where the child becomes aware of body parts as we discussed earlier. The focus of terror is commonly blood. At this age a child wants a band-aid for any injury, real or supposed. A band-aid makes everything better. The child believes the band-aid will stop the blood from leaving their body. Fear of pain is also very common. If the child isn't worried about losing blood, he is focused on the immense pain from that shot (this is the same shot that he didn't flinch at six months ago). Simply because he has entered this developmental age level, he is perceiving life and its events differently than before. Do not feed into this hysteria. Remind him that six months ago the shot didn't hurt; he was so brave.

The fear of injury to the body is a concern. If the child breaks any item, it is likely that he will react disproportionately. A broken toy becomes the end of the world. He responds to this as if he'll never see another one like it. When a puzzle has missing pieces, it is "broken" and cannot be repaired. He will not want to work the puzzle again unless it can be fixed. The child is not being defiant in doing this; he is sincerely bothered and upset that the item is broken. The child may respond in horror if he sees a headless doll. Once again, not due to violence of decapitation, but rather it is "broken".

When responding to these fears, encourage the child's independence in thought and action, although you still need to monitor him. Teach him safety rules (never talk to strangers, develop a safety code word to use in an emergency if you need to send someone to pick him up from school). The child must learn his home telephone number and address (and last name, of course). Practice mommy's work number. Remind him that you are responsible for protecting him but that you really need his help in making sure that he remains safe. Let your child know that it takes both to make this happen. Practice saying "no". Role-play situation that involve yelling "no" and running for help.

By allowing the child to experience trial-and-error moments, he develops confidence. Allow him to make some of his own choices. Whenever possible, give him a choice of two or three items he'd rather do. Let him choose his preference. Follow through with his choice. I have observed parents with the best intentions to doing this, but at the last moment they would choose an option different than the child.

Example:

Parent: What do you want for dinner tonight Tyler? We have the following leftovers: baked chicken, fried fish, or a roast sandwich.

Tyler: A sandwich.

Parent: Okay. I guess I'll heat up some chicken for you.

There is a problem. Why did the parent ask the child's preference when there was no intention on following through? Giving the child chicken when he chose a sandwich totally undermines the purpose of giving choices. The child's chance at independence was crushed. Once again, his choice was not addressed.

It is also important that you reassure the child that just because he tries to accomplish something and fails at it, that he is not "bad". Our children learn the words "good" and "bad" early. Society rates everything as good or bad. Children rate themselves and their actions accordingly. Reassuring the child that he is not "bad" because he ran over the garden hose with his bicycle is important. The word "accidental" needs to be taught to our children as early as they can understand the meaning. We sure do not want to raise a child mired in guilt and exhibiting low self-esteem due to a lack of independence and rare reinforcement.

At four years of age, children often exhibit a behavior called boasting. When they boast, it is in a verbal play mode. The parents should not take this very seriously. The child will say, "I live in the biggest house ever."

"My daddy is better than anyone."

"My dog is the best ever." Boasting can be utilized as a form of verbal reinforcement to eliminate fears.

When the child discusses, "I am the bravest knight ever," it would be prudent to take the time to talk with him about how the bravest knight could rid the kingdom of the monster's. Let the child develop the monster characteristics and legend (you don't want to add to his fears by suggesting horrific details). Join him in discussing how he, as the knight, can eradicate the "badness" because he's so good and clever. Give him confidence. Let him know that monsters are so afraid of knights like him that they probably have left for good knowing that he was on to them. Join the child in the boasts and imagination to create many optimal solutions for the fears he may have. Encourage his faith in himself.

Between the ages of two and six the child is more likely to experience strange and sometimes violent fears. Although these are a passing phase, they must be addressed with care and thought. Comforting and understanding the child, his perspective, and his confusion are important. Once again, never shame, dismiss, nor scold him due to these.

The University Society (1970) identifies two types of fear. The first is a normal fear, which is born from a dangerous or frightening situation. If a dog has bitten a child, it is realistic for the child to be afraid of this event repeating itself with all dogs. If a child choked on a piece of fish, it is logical that he may be afraid of eating fish again. The second type of fear is anxiety. This fear is related to a deep emotion, an uneasiness, within. Sometimes the child doesn't know why he is worrying, or believes he is worried about one thing when actually it is caused by something else. This is also found in adults. A person believes they are worried about a lack of communication in their marriage when the real point of concern is the trust level. Children are like this on a lighter scale.

A child in this age range is very small and vulnerable. He is dependent upon his parents or caregivers. Separation anxiety is normal at age two. Will Mommy ever come back to pick me up? Has she forgotten me? Sometimes the child believes that he is responsible for parents separating. "I was so bad...I didn't eat my spinach or clean my room. That's why Daddy left." Although this is not logical to the adults, and we may never consider the existence of these thoughts within our child, they do occur, and not infrequently. When conducting family therapy following a familial restructuring, I often talk to the children individually. The majority of the time, at least one child will feel responsible for the split. The small mistakes a child makes, he often holds accountable for larger life crisis.

At age two, most children are afraid of: being left alone, pain and injury, animals, people who don't act or look as those the child is used to, and death. They don't understand new or novel experiences that may startle them. The parent needs to be aware of these possible fears and be proactive. Before the tears take hold and begin to grow, try to address them. Reassure the child that if you leave you will return. Let the child see you petting non-dangerous animals and encourage him/her to do the same in your company. The other fears can be addressed through demystifying each one. Death, pain and injury are scary because they are unknown. We never see people smiling or happy while encountering them. Discuss this with the child .

Building Self-Esteem

"I may as well not even apply for that job; who would hire me anyway?"

"I don't bother to take care with my appearance. It can't change who I am...miserable."

"I stay with my boyfriend even though he hurts me because we both know I cannot get anyone better."

Self-esteem, as defined by Nathan Branden (1994) is "the experience that we are appropriate to life and to the requirements of life. This involves (1) confidence in our ability to think, confidence in our ability to cope with the basic challenges of life, and (2) confidence in our right to be successful and happy, the feeling of being worthy, deserving, entitled to assert out needs and wants, achieve our values, and enjoy the fruits of our efforts." This is a complete definition of self-esteem; it is much more in depth and easier to comprehend than the vague, often offered, "self-worth" definition.

True self-esteem is internal and external. It impacts all aspects of our lives. When a person experiences poor self-esteem, he is likely to also show irritability, irrational behavior, fear of the new and unknown, defensiveness, resistance to change, and hostility toward others. When one has positive self-esteem, they are open to life and its possibilities. People are no longer a threat. Events are not competitive. Life is composed of conflicts and crisis. Positive self-esteem gives us the flexibility to approach life's struggles without predisposed bias. We are able to employ new and creative solutions to old problems. We know that our opinions and beliefs have value and this gives us the confidence and encouragement to express them. So many aspects of the quality of life are tied to one's level of self-esteem. How we perceive life is how we respond to it.

A person will act as they feel. When you are ill, you act like you do not feel well. Your response time is slower, your energy is drained, and not much thought or effort is put into your attire. Self-esteem is no different; when a person has low self-esteem, they believe they are not worthy and that they are substandard. As we noted above, this affects the way we treat and respond to others. The first change that must be made in the quest to build self-esteem is to change the way one feels. Thus, the actions will follow.

We have discussed the power of positive thinking and how to learn cognitive restructuring. It is now time to implement these strategies. The positive thought should be affirming, valid and realistic, and it should show the overused negative thought to be a lie. Write down your negative thought. Rate the intensity of the negative thought, 1-10 (1= not very negative, 10= extremely negative). Write down the emotions that accompany this negative thought (happy, sad, discouraged, frustrated, angry, lonely, guilty, anxious, fearful, manipulated, inferior, etc.) Rate each emotion's intensity as well, using the same scale. From this emotion intensity breakdown, write a positive thought.

Example:

Negative thought: My boyfriend and I have separated. I feel lonely and useless.

Emotions and intensities: sad 40%, discouraged 40%, lonely 90%, angry 40%, manipulated 90%, frustrated 80%

Positive thoughts: I do not feel inferior although I am lonely.

I am not fearful because I can make my own decisions and I know what is right for me.

I am angry because I feel used and manipulated; I am smart enough to see through guys like this.

The next time I date someone, I will not fall as easily for his games. I will be aware.

These are affirmation statements that are true and realistic. The individual does not state that she will be the most popular girl on the social scene just because she is single. She does not state that she will date the most sought-after partner and will "show the ex" what he is missing. These statements are not revenge based; they center on the individual's qualities of self. Capitalize on the strengths. This exercise will be difficult in the beginning if the self-esteem is low. Practice makes it easier. The distorted thinking must be changed into valid and realistic, positive thinking.

Low self-esteem encourages the individual to accept faulty information as true. When we fell negatively about ourselves, and someone else says we are inept, we are likely to accept this as true. Why? If this same someone were to walk up and state, "Puff the magic dragon is sitting at the mall", you wouldn't believe him. Consider the statement. Consider the source. If the person actually believed you to be inept, why would he bother telling you anything? Why would he waste time talking about you at all? The evidence does not support the allegation. This statement cannot be accepted as true and valid.

This is also true for negative self-statements. These are to be completely outlawed and never allowed. These are so unfair. The speaker (you) never compliments, only criticizes which makes the process off-balance. If it is off-balance, it should not be considered as true or valid. By the same token, if you only compliment yourself and never critique, this is also off-balance. If you begin to doubt the truth of a self-statement, create an experiment to confirm or deny your hypothesis. Survey your friends for their opinions.

Confronting your negative thoughts, restating them in a more positive format, then allowing yourself to own and accept them is another option. I have had the honor of working with some incredible therapists in this business. One of the best, who does marriage therapy and women's issues, ascribes to the acceptance approach. She has integrated her fear into the whole personality replete with numerous strengths.

"I can feel insecure about certain things, express this concern, and then realize I own it. It is part of who I am." Her strengths of problem solving and long-term goal setting help her align her sporadic and current fears. Her security concerns are based on reality. She does not allow them to grow beyond what she can manage. She does not allow the anxiety to alter her thinking nor direction. She accepts that she has this anxiety and prefers top use it as a monitor of safety.

Low self-esteem can sabotage romantic aspects of one's life as well. When the low self-esteem is present, the individual becomes either clingy or distant and cold. When clingy, the person is terrified the loved one will leave. By virtually stalking the person, they belief they are showing love and concern. Calling the individual numerous times during the workday is considered an example of passion not a barrage of interruptions that could get the person fired. When the individual with low self-esteem opts to pull away, it is often out of fear and dread. Afraid that the relationship will soon be over, he/she begins to pull away, anticipating what is believed to be the inevitable. This individual is certain that he/she is unlovable and if the other hasn't figured that to be so they will soon. Past experiences of pain have taught this person that they will always lose in love so they should expect it. Actually, he/she is running off the loved one by pulling away. This will hasten the break-up.

When we know we are doomed, we act in ways that make sure we are. If a person is working at a job they cannot successfully perform, they often initiate their own dismissal. A secretary may hide important files and authorizations, an accountant may create a dummy account and funnel money to it, or a supervisor may refuse to train his employees because he is afraid they will realize his shortcomings. In all cases, the people are trying to protect themselves by outing themselves. The question I ask is if these people are aware of their lack of knowledge why not address this problem by gaining the knowledge needed? Each has a low self-esteem, believing them unable to learn to perform.

Look at each individual's personal life. Is the person in an equal relationship or is the partner the aggressor? Is there honesty in the relationship or is the individual hiding information there as well? Low self-esteem affects all areas of our existence.

The development of self-esteem begins in childhood. In order to examine the origins of low self-esteem it is prudent to begin with the parents. Was the individual's mother passive, aggressive, or passive aggressive? How did the child interact wit the mother? Was the child held accountable for his/her own actions? Was there violence or abuse in the home? If so, what kinds? Was the child a direct or indirect victim of this? Traumatic situations that occurred in childhood should be examined. The earliest memory of the individual should be documented. What fears did the person have when young? What were the origins of the fears?

Looking at the interaction with other family members is important. Siblings, even extended family members can play a part in the value one places on the self. How were the early years of school? Were there bullies who antagonized the person? To what degree? When a child is in elementary school, self-esteem development is in high gear. By first grade, there is a popular crowd and the outsiders. Imagine what a first grader must feel when she wants to eat lunch with peers and they move away. We don't often consider childhood cruelty beginning so early, but it is rampant. Talk to your child's teacher and guidance counselor concerning this. Ask how your child interacts with peers and vice versa. Keep on top of this.

Look into the individual's history of interpersonal relationships as a teen and an adult. Is there a pattern? If the woman has low self-esteem, a pattern is often present.

Example:

The father left the family when the girl was nine. The mother didn't hesitate to remind her, "You were too much trouble; that's why he left." As a teen, she tried to hang on to any boy who would look at her, often trading sex for company. As an adult, she chased married men, throwing herself at them because she wanted the attention but knew they would be safer than most since they were attached. She wanted the company but didn't want the man. She chased what she couldn't have in order to not obtain it. She is repeatedly proving to herself that her individual worth is negative. This cycle will repeat itself until she changes one element...her view of her own worth.

Some people enter into abusive relationships, where they are dependent on another for all elements of existence, because this is all they know. They were abused as children and on some level, believe they deserved the abuse then and now. The excuses she heard as a child, "He didn't mean to do it, " "He really does love us even though he hurts us," become her adult reality. This is a world she knows. She may not like it, but it is nothing new. The verbal abuse that accompanies the other types serves to reinforce her self-esteem that was destroyed as a child. This basic pattern of self-destruction continues.

Inadequate self-esteem results in a bad mate choice, a missed job promotion, even a sabotaged profession. The individual is stagnant. Nathaniel Branden, author of *Six Pillars of Self-Esteem*, lists the six factors he identifies as the foundations of self-esteem:

- The practice of living consciously

- The practice of self-acceptance

- The practice of self-responsibility

- The practice of self-assertiveness

- The practice of living purposefully

- The practice of personal integrity

In summary, he suggests that living consciously is living responsibly toward reality. We must recognize what we see to be what it really is, not as we wish it to be. Self-acceptance is (1) being self-affirming, (2) being real to ourselves about what we feel, desire, have done and what we are, and (3) showing compassion while taking responsibility. Self-responsibility for one's actions and goal attainment at the third pillar. Self-assertiveness is the ability to honor one's wants, values and needs and expressing these in an appropriate manner within society. This is not aggression. To live purposefully is to use one's abilities for goal attainment. Your life has a purpose; make it happen. Integrity is defined as the integration of ideals, convictions, standards of beliefs and behavior. When one acts in a manner that causes conflict between what they know is moral (integrity) and what they impulsively want to do, a personal crisis will develop. Practicing personal integrity means doing the right thing even if you don't want to at the moment.

Abraham Maslow (1970) developed a theory utilizing the Hierarchy of Needs. He developed this hierarchy to show what individual needs must be met before the next is possible to achieve. At the base of this diagram are the physiological needs such as water, oxygen, and food. If a child is hungry, he cannot focus on much else. As this need is satisfied, the safety needs are in question. The individual needs to feel safe, secure, and stable in their world. Without a sense of security in our lives, how do we plan for a future? Belongingness and love needs are next. Humans have the need to love and be loved, to belong and be accepted by others. We avoid loneliness and alienation, as this is counterproductive to our growth. Esteem needs are the next to be met. Once physiological needs, safety needs, belongingness and love needs have been satisfied, one feels confident enough to develop self-esteem. This is a need for achievement, competence, and independence. We have a need in this level for recognition and respect from others as well. These reinforce our self-esteem. The final stage of the hierarchy is the self-actualization need. This is when we have the need to maximize our potential. When we become what we always knew we could, when we have realized our fullest abilities, we are self-actualized. Maslow shows that self-esteem is not easily developed not destroyed. To own a positive self-esteem, one must work at it. It should be carefully tended and reinforced.

Utilize the information presented in this book to develop a positive self-esteem. This is really the basis for confronting anxieties and fears. When one has faith in the self and abilities therein, negativity has a hard time braking through that positive fortress. The time to begin these exercises is now. Too long have you spent at the receiving end of others' who are all too anxious to criticize and demean you. When their self-esteem is low, some people mistakenly and illogically believe that verbally (and sometimes physically) attacking others will make them appear superior. Prepubescent girls are masters at this. They identify an attractive, intelligent girl at their school. Realizing that if this girl was to understand her strengths and attributes, the other girls may not be the most popular anymore. Their objective: demean and destroy. This way she will not be a threat.

We'd like to think that adults are too old to play these ridiculous games. We all know this to be a fallacy. Adults can be just as venomous as the young girls. Both are similarly defeated by a positive self-esteem. Remember that no one can make you feel or believe anything you do not choose. To combat this onslaught, just say "no". Choose not to participate. A game cannot be played by only one side. Choosing not to play, but rather reveling in your positive self-esteem, utilizing your pillars and hierarchies for certain achievements and success, you automatically win. The self-appointed adversaries do not have the skills you possess. Their strategies are flawed with fallacies. These people eventually wither and dry up if they continue this approach. You, on the other hand, will be a winner.

Reference Page

Ainsworth, M. D. S., Blehar, M. C., Waters, E., & Wall, S. (1978). *Patterns of attachment: A psychological study of the strange situation.* Hillsdale, NJ: Erlbaum.

Ainsworth, M. (1982). Attachment: retrospect and prospect. In: CM Parkes & J. Stevenson-Hinde (eds.) The place of attachment in human behaviour. New York: Basic Books.

Amato, P. R., & Keith, B. (1991). Parental divorce and the well-being of children: Ameta-analysis. *Psychological Bulletin, 110,* 26-46.

Antonovsky, A. (1979). *Health, stress, and coping.* San Francisco: Jossey-Bass.

Aust, P. H. (1981). Using the life story book in treatments of children in placement. *Child Welfare, 60*(8), 535-560.

Backhaus, K. A. (1984). Life books: Tools for working with children in placement. *Social Work, 29,* 551-554.

Balon,R., Pohl, R., Yeragami, V. K., Rainey, J. M., & Berchou, R. (1988). Follow-up study of control subjects with lactate-and isoproterenol-induced panic attacks. *American Journal of Psychiatry, 145,* 238-241.

Barrett, R. K. (1995). *Children mourning mourning children.* Kenneth J. Doka, (Ed.). Washington, DC: Hospice Foundation of America.

Barnard, C. P. & Corrales, R. C. (1979). *The therapy and technique of family therapy.* (2nd ed.). Springfield, Illinois: Charles C. Thomas.

Bartholomew, K. (1990). Avoidance of intimacy: An attachment perspective. *Journal of Social and Personal Relationships, 7,* 147-178.

Blanchard, M., & Main, M. (1979). Avoidance of the attachment figure and social-emotional adjustment in day-care Infants. *Developmental Psychology, 15,* 445-446.

Bowen, M. (1976). Principles and Techniques of Multiple Family Therapy in *FamilyTherapy: Theory and Practice,* edited by P. J. Guerin. New York: GardnerPress.

Bowlby, J. (1961). *Attachment and loss.* Vols. 1 and 2. New York: Basic Books.

Bowlby, J. (1970). *Attachment: Loss.* New York: Basic Books.

Bowlby, J. (1973). *Separation: Anxiety and anger.* New York: Basic Books.

Branden, N. (1994). *Six pillars of self-esteem.* New York: Bantam Books.

Briggs, R. (2005). Moving from fear to freedom. Excerpted from *TransformingAnxiety, Transcending Shame,* retrieved from the World Wide Web on September12, 2005 at http://www.eNotAlone.com.

Burney, R. (1995). *The dance of the wounded souls.* Excerpt, *Reprogramming ourdysfunctional ego defenses,* retrieved form the World Wide Web on September 1,2005 at http://Joy2MeU.com.

Corsini, R. J. (1995). *Current psychotherapies.* Illinois: F. E. Peacock Publishers, Inc.

Crowell, J., Fraley, R. C., & Shaver, P. R. (1999). Measures of individual differencesin adolescent and adult attachment, In J. Cassidy & P. R. Shaver (Eds.),*Handbook of attachment: Theory, research, and clinical applications.* NewYork: Guilford Press.

Dollard, J. & Miller, N. E. (1950). *Personality and psychotherapy.* New York:McGraw-Hill Book Company, Inc.

Drummond, E. H. (1997). *Overcoming anxiety without tranquilizers: Agroundbreaking program for treating chronic anxiety.* New York, NY: PenguinBooks.

Epstein,S. (1972). The nature of anxiety with its emphasis upon its relationship toexpectancy. In C.D. Spielberger (Ed.), *Anxiety: Current trends in theory andresearch* (Vol. 2). New York: Academic Press.

Erikson, E. H. (1963). *Childhood and society.* New York: Norton.

Fraley, R. C., & Shaver, P. R. (in press). Adult romantic attachment: Theoreticaldevelopments, emerging controversies, and unanswered questions. *Review ofGeneral Psychology.*

Freud, S. (1936). *The problem of anxiety.* New York: W. W. Norton & Company.

Ghabi, J. (2000). *Living in fear.* Retrieved from the World Wide Web on September 30,2005, from http:www.freespiritcentre.info.

Great Quotations, Inc. (2002). *Motivating quotes for motivated people.* Hong Kong:Great Quotations Publishing Co.

Grossman, H. (1966). *Teaching the emotionally disturbed: A casebook.* New York:Holt, Rinehart, and Winston, Inc.

Harrison, J., Campbell, E., & Chumbley, P. (1987). *Making history: A social worker'sguide to lifebooks.* Frankfurt: Kentucky Cabinet for Human Services,Department of Social Services.

Haynes, P. & Mabray, D. (2006). *Deployment: A Family Affair.* PublishAmerica.

Hazan, C., & Shaver, P. (1987). Romantic love conceptualized as an attachmentprocess. *Journal of Personality and Social Psychology, 52,* 511-524.

Hetherington, E. M., & Clingempeel, W. G. (1992). Coping with marital transitions: Afamily systems perspective. *Society for Research in Child DevelopmentMonographs, 57,* 1-242.

Hetherington, E. M., Reiss, D., & Plomin, R. (1993). *The separate social worlds ofsiblings: The impact of nonshared environment on development.* Hillsdale, NJ:Erlbaum.

Janis, I. (1971). *Stress and frustration.* New York: Harcourt, Brace, & World.

Jung, C. G. (1939). *The integration of personality.* New York: Farrar & Rinehart.

Junginger, J. & Turner, S. M. (1987). Spontaneous exposure and "self-control" in thetreatment of obsessive checking.

Journal of Behavior Therapy and ExperimentalPsychiatry, 18, 115-119.

Kaufman, J., & Ziggler, E. (1987). Do abused children become abusive parents? *American Journal of Orthopsychiatry, 57,* 186-192.

Kempe, R. S., & Kempe, C. C. (1978). *Child abuse.* Cambridge, MA: HarvardUniversity Press.

Kempe, C. H., & Helfer, R. E. (1972). *Helping the battered child and his family.* USA:J. B. Lippincott Company.

Kendall-Tackett, K. A., Williams, L. M., & Finkelhor, D. (1993). Impact of sexualabuse on children: A review and synthesis of recent empirical studies. *Psychological Bulletin, 113,* 164-180.

Kohlberg, L. (1981). *The philosophy of moral development: Essays on moraldevelopment* (Vol. 1). San Francisco: Harper & Row.

Lazarus, R. S. (1966). *Patterns of adjustment and human effectiveness.* New York:McGraw Hill.

Leach, P. (1978). *Your baby and child: From birth to age five.* NY: Alfred A. Knopf.

Lewis, D. O., Pincus, J. H., Bard, B., Richardson, E., Prichep, I. S., Feldman, M., &Yeager, C. (1988). Neuropsychiatric psycho educational, and familycharacteristics of 14 juveniles condemned to death in the United States. *American Journal of Psychiatry, 145,* 584-589.

Lindsay, W. R., Gamisu, C. V., McLaughlin, E., Hood, E. M., & Espie, C. A. (1987). A controlled trial of treatments for generalized anxiety. *British Journal of Clinical Psychology,* 26, 3-15.

Mabray, D. & LaBauve, B. (currently in press). *Let's Talk: Communicating with YourChild.*

Mabray, D. (2004). *The ultimate study guide for psychological theories.* Texas:ACFCC Publishing.

Mabray, D. (2004). *The ultimate study guide for marriage and family theories.* Texas:ACFCC Publishing.

Malinosky-Rummell, R., & Hansen, D. J. (1993). Longterm consequences of childhoodphysical abuse. *Psychological Bulletin, 114,* 68-74.

Maxmen, J. S., & Ward, N. G. (1995). *Essential psychopathology and its treatment.* 2nd edition. NY: W. W. Norton & Co.

Mineka, S., & Suomi, S. J. (1978). Social separation in monkeys. *PsychologicalBulletin, 85,* 1376-1400.

Moore, J. D. (2005). *Overcoming fear, uncertainty and doubt.* Retrieved from theWorld Wide Web on June 6, 2005 at http://www.eNotAlone.com.

Myers, D. G. *Psychology,* 4th ed. New York, NY: Worth Publishers.

National Center for Health Statistics. (1991). Family structure and children's health:United States, 1988. *Vital and health statistics,* Series 10, No. 178, DHHSPublication No. PHS 91-1506 by Deborah A. Dawson.

Oregon State Extension Service. (1993). *Handling children's fears.* Reprinted byCindee Bailey, Oregon: Oregon State University .

Passman, R. H. (1987). Attachments to inanimate objects: Are children who havesecurity blankets insecure? *Journal of Counseling & Clinical Psychology, 55,*825-830.

Piaget, J. (1952). *The origins of Intelligence in children.* New York: InternationalUniversities Press.

Piantanida, M., & Anderson, S. (1990). *Creating and using lifebooks: A guide foradoptive parents.* Pittsburgh: Three Rivers Adoption Council.

Price, J. M. (1934). *Personal factors in character building.* Nashville, Tenn.: TheSunday School Board of the Southern Baptist Convention.

Rachman, S. (1974). *The meaning of fear.* Middlesex, England: Penguin Books.

Rogers, C. R. (1951). *Client-centered therapy.* Boston: Houghton Mifflin Company.

Rogers, C. R. (1980). *A way of being.* Boston: Houghton Mifflin.

Rutter, M. (1979). Maternal deprivation, 1972-1978: New findings, new concepts, newapproaches. *Child Development, 50,* 283-305.

Schurman, C. (2005). *Fear: O psychological obstacles to performance.* Retrieved fromthe Wide World Web on October 3, 2005 at http://www.bodyresults.com.

Sears, R. R., Maccoley, E. E., & Levin, H. (1957). *Patterns of childrearing.* NewYork: Harper & Row.

Seifer, R., Schiller, M., Sameroff, A. J., Resnick, S., & Riordan, K. (1996). Attachment, maternal sensitivity, and infant temperament during the first year of life. *Developmental Psychology, 32,* 12-25.

Smith, M. B. (1949). Combat motivations among ground troops. In S. A. Stouffer (Ed.), *The American soldier.* Princeton, NJ: Princeton University Press.

Spock, B. (1976). *Baby and child care.* New York, NY: Pocket Books, Simon & Schuster, Inc.

Sue, D., Sue, D., & Sue, S. (1990). *Understanding abnormal behavior.* (3rd ed.). NewJersey: Houghton Mifflin Company.

Sullivan, H. S. (1953). *The interpersonal theory of psychiatry.* New York: W. W. Norton & Company, Inc.

The University Society, Incorporated. (1970). *Infant and child care.* Midland Park, NJ:The University Society, Inc.

Thompson, R. A., Lamb, M. E., & Estes, D. (1982). Stability of infant-motherattachment and its relationship to changing life circumstances in an unselectedmiddle-class sample. *Child Development, 53,* 144-148.

Wallerstein, J. S. (1991). The long-term effects of divorce on children: A review. *Journal of the American Academy of Child and Adolescent Psychiatry, 30,* 349-360.

Widom, C. S. (1989). Does violence begat violence? A critical examination of theliterature. *Psychological Bulletin, 106,* 3-28.

_____. *Attachment styles in romantic love.* Retrieved from the
World Wide Web onSeptember 1, 2005 at http://www.about.com.

_____. (2004). *Challenging fear into amazing success.*
Retrieved from the WorldWide Web on August 15, 2005 at http:/
/www.PowerfulThings.com.

_____. *Handling our emotions.* Retrieved from the World
Wide Web on August30, 2005, http://www.KidsEQ.com.

_____.*Overcome fear of failure and enjoy pushing yourself.*
Retrieved from theWorld Wide Web on August 23, 2005, http//
:www.HypnosisDownloads.com.

Printed in the United States
53292LVS00002B/178-234

9 781424 132416